SURVIVING THE DATING GAME

SURVIVING THE DATING GAME

Secrets A Woman
Should Know

SURPAUL COTTRELL

SECRET 1

How to Make a Relationship Work

How do you make a relationship work? There are many things both parties need to do, and the first is the necessary homework. This consists of first learning about your man or woman. Find out what his or her interests are. What types of food does he or she enjoy? What types of food and dessert does he or she dislike? Does your partner like going to plays and watching musicals? Is he or she into music? If so, what's his or her favorite, and what's the least favorite type of music?

You have to dig deep if you want the relationship to flow smoothly. Communication

If communication does not exist, then there is no relationship. Ask your partner how he or she is doing today. "How are you feeling?" or "Is there anything on your mind you would like to talk about?" are some of the essential questions to ask your significant other throughout your relationship.

Trust is a huge part in a relationship. Trust is also a great part of communication. If you can't trust your lover, how can you let that person in on your personal feelings on sensitive subjects? If you don't trust your man or woman, then you need to sever the relationship instantly.

Showing Affection

To get to the bottom of who is more affectionate in relationships, I interviewed a variety of men and women. In analyzing the results of these casual conversations, I feel that the women turned out to be more affectionate.

Men can be very affectionate, but not always at the times their partners need them to be. For example, it's 3:00 am. You've had a few drinks. Crawling into bed with your lover can be a poor choice. It might be a weeknight; he may have to work in the morning. He may need some rest, but you won't let him get any. And even though your libido may be at its highest, "I'm not in the mood," and "Baby, I got to go to work tomorrow" still means *no*. After the first time he ignores you, give up and satisfy yourself. Just remember that pleasing yourself while your partner is trying to get some sleep can also be a problem. It can go well, but there's always the possibility that it can go sour. I'll begin with the good: Depending on the type of individual your lover is, your activity may actually cause his libido to awaken—and now you may have a chance at reaching your climax. On the other hand, he may question your judgment and manners or even think that you need mental help.

Honesty

Dishonesty is one of the top reasons relationships and marriages fail. When you are with someone, that individual is also supposed to be your best friend. You are not supposed to keep any secrets from your lover, no matter what. It can always blow up in your face at a later date.

It could be the littlest thing to you, but you can't predict how your lover will react to the deception. Imagine being at work and a co-worker comes on to you. From the very start, you let this person know that you are not interested in stepping outside of your relationship. But for some odd reason, the more you speak about your significant other, the more that only intensifies their attempts to seduce you in the office.

What do you do at this point?
Do you tell your significant other?
Do you keep this to yourself?

For starters, remember to tell your lover everything. This person that you are not in a relationship with is acting out of character. If this person keeps acting insane, it could lead to other things. If they don't get what they want whether that is sex or for you and your lover to break up), then things could get out of hand and lead to sexual harassment charges.

A domestic violence charge is usually accompanied by a restraining order. Imagine being charged with this—and just because you chose to keep silent, you find yourself in trouble at home, too. If you had told the person you are in a relationship with about the unwanted advances of your co-worker, he or she may have had a solution for you. But now, you may find your relationship damaged over rumors and lies created by this deranged individual. If that's not a great reason to be honest, in your eyes, then you don't belong in a relationship.

There are also smaller things that also matter when it comes to honesty. When your partner asks for your opinion, whether it's on the shirt they are wearing, the food they are preparing, or their plans for the evening, always answer these simple questions honestly. If not, you may pay for it in the future.

Get to Know Your Companion Spiritually

To know your companion spiritually, you really don't have to be a religious individual. Knowing what your lover believes in and what religion they follow is important. What exactly does it entail? You and your lover may not share a common belief system. Your lover may even believe in something that you or your families are totally against. It's important to have this discussion at the very beginning of your relationship. If not, the deep conflicts that you have not discussed could be problematic down the line.

You may be so deeply in love that you just put up with certain things because you are comfortable with your beau. (I'll speak more on this a little later on in the book.) It's a great feeling when the two of you can sit and pray together for peace and happiness. If the spiritual side of things is important to you, this might be a nice bonding experience for you. Give it a try at least once.

Be Adventurous

In a relationship, you have to be ready to challenge yourself. Find out the things that your significant other is extremely interested in. You may find that a certain activity or interest might challenge your idea of what is gender-appropriate for your partner, but try to have an open mind. It may not be your cup of tea, but at least try to respect that it's something your lover loves. Aren't you interested in why a certain activity brings them happiness? Whether it's going to a play or a museum or trying snorkeling or even just having a picnic, would it *really* hurt you to try something new?

How would you feel if you were shot down every time you asked your partner to join you in one of your hobbies or interests? Hearing nothing but "no" or "I'm not interested" or "I promised myself I would never do that" can cripple a relationship. I know that I would feel like my relationship was at a standstill if neither of us ever agreed to try new things. There are no rules in the dating game that prohibit you from asking people you know about the type of special things they do with their partners. Do your research.

Commitment

A commitment is an obligation or a promise, and yes, an engagement is one type of commitment. Being "committed" is not the same thing as being "engaged." What it means is that you need commitment to make a relationship work. Day to day, you have to implement self-control. Every handsome man or beautiful woman who crosses your path should not have you lusting. Without self-control, you could easily become a lothario and a cheater each time an attractive person threw him- or herself at you.

I know that it is hard to turn this sort of proposition down, especially when you don't have to put any effort into getting him or her behind closed doors. To be honest with you, stepping outside of your relationship today is far from safe. New diseases are being discovered all the time. Imagine meeting the perfect individual at a nightclub. Add a few too many drinks, kisses, and bad decisions into the mix, and before you know it, you're in trouble. You might have contracted a disease you could carry for the rest of your life.

How would you feel if your lover brought home such a "gift"? Would you be forgiving if they brought something that hazardous into your relationship? Would you appreciate being given some other partner's disease, one that gives you an excruciating burning sensation each time you urinate? Don't feel that because you are using protection, everything is tranquil. Prophylactics are not 100 percent safe. If they are not properly used, they won't protect you—and that could cut your life—and that of your partner—short, just because you stepped outside of your relationship. Mother used to say, "Better safe than sorry." Stay committed to your lover and your relationship. Stay healthy. Remember, no relationship is perfect.

Satisfying Your Man or Woman

If you are not doing this correctly, it could destroy your relationship. If you are not sure what satisfies your significant other, you'd better find out as soon as possible. There are ways to satisfy somebody you are with, besides sexually. A great way to know that your lover is happy is to look to see if they smile when you do something for them. Sometimes it helps to do special things that the average person would have to put their mind to. How would you feel if you just got out of the shower after a horrible day at work to find a surprise waiting for you in the bed?

When you pull the covers back, you find a Christian Dior and a Louis Vuitton box filled with different items. Two weeks later, you enter your vehicle in the morning and discover a Barney's New York shopping bag with a couple of items in it—the very items you told your sister you wanted a few days ago. Wouldn't that make you smile?

Sometimes you have to think outside of the box to put a smile on your man or woman's face. It doesn't hurt to brainstorm on certain things that could keep a smile on a person's face. Some women out there wouldn't mind getting roses delivered to their workplace once a week. Some men would love a high-end bottle of cologne delivered to their workplace twice a month (so that they can smell good for you, of course). You can do the rose petals and candlelit dinner thing, but put your spin on it; make it yours. You have to put your mind to it. Think how many guys are doing the same thing. Think about all the ladies repeating the same thing.

There's no originality anymore. Everything is starting to seem a lot like music these days, repetitive. A lot of fashion is also being repeated. Be original.

Sexuality

A man and a woman can only take the same thing over and over so many times. You have to switch your moves sometimes. If you feel that your man or woman is doing something wrong, it doesn't hurt to get a professional video and study it. Nobody is perfect. The person you are with can be the most beautiful person to you, but if their bedroom game is below average, that's a bad hit. You can only fake an orgasm for so long. I really don't think that it's cool to fake an orgasm at all.

If you are trying to make a relationship work, you have to be honest all the time (even if your partner has an awful odor protruding from their private area). No matter what it is, you have to be honest with yourself and your partner. Do you want this relationship to work? Are you willing to do anything and everything to make this relationship work? Ask yourself these questions before you continue.

SECRET 2

The Rebound

An astronomical number of women become victims of "the rebound" during vulnerable times. There are a number of ways a woman can become the rebound. The "rebounded" doesn't necessarily have to be a woman. A lot of men also become the rebounded.

Here are a few examples of how you can earn this hideous label. Have you ever been infatuated with a man or a woman? They know exactly how you feel, but they completely blow you off. Every time you call them, it's a different excuse. After several phone calls and messages, you start to get fed up with getting treated like a red-headed stepchild. Suddenly, your phone rings and this person finally sends you a tweet or instant message telling you that he or she would love to hook up with you.

At this point, you are so shocked that this person finally took the time to reach out to you that you give in. You're a weak individual. What happens now? Let's look at two scenarios.

Example Number One

In the first scenario, you hook up with the man or woman. The two of you go on a date. Then, at the end of the night, he or she invites you to his or her apartment. You decide to turn the offer down. Even though part of you wanted to go, another part of you wanted to take things slowly. What usually happens here? They may never call you again because you didn't sleep with them. If you really put your mind to it, you'll realize that they only got in contact with you because—more than likely—you were the only option available.

And guess what that makes you?

Answer: the rebound.

Example Number Two

You choose to go to his or her apartment at the end of the night. You end up kissing this individual passionately, but then you stop in the middle of everything. You tell them that you can't do anything more. You inform them that you are hemorrhaging profusely. After you realize that you have confused your partner for the night, you explain that you are having menstrual cramps and you don't think the two of you should continue.

What happens next?

They come up with some type of excuse to get you out of their apartment. In their mind, they are wondering, *Why you didn't tell me from the beginning that you were having cramps?*

Guess what happens now? They'll probably never call you again. *Why?* Because you were just the rebound.

Example Number Three

After suffering a devastating breakup, the victim decided to post a blog on his or her web page about the situation. You don't know the individual from a hole in the wall, but the picture at the end of their blog turns you on. You contact them. As the weeks pass, the two of you begin cyber dating (dating on the Internet).

Finally, you end up meeting with him or her a few times. After a few encounters, the two of you have sexual relations a number of times.

You start to realize that you really have feelings for this person, and you just can't believe how strong they are becoming. Now you want to start seeing him or her every day. As the days fly by, you start to see a dramatic difference in the amount of time the two of you are spending with one another. And then you begin to notice the other person is throwing you on the back burner.

Finally, you decide to ask what's going on. The person tells you that the person he or she broke up with is trying to work things out again.

So where does that leave you?

Answer: Remember, "I love you" doesn't mean anything if it's not offered sincerely. And once again, you were just the rebound.

Example Number Four

You are in a downtown bar, clubbing and having a blast. You become disappointed when the clubbing comes to an end. It's early, you don't have to work tomorrow, and it's your birthday. Someone at the bar asks you what you want to do, and you explain that you have no plans. The next thing you know, the person gets a phone call. The audio from the phone call is extremely loud and clear.

You hear the person on the other end of the phone tell your friend that they are severely inebriated and have to cancel their plans. When the call is over, your new friend asks you if you want to hang out.

What do you do in this situation? Do you avoid being the rebound?

Answer: It's totally up to you. If you leave with him or her, you will become a statistic to the rebound. After viewing the following examples, you should have a general understanding for the definition of "the rebound." It's a fall-back plan.

It's not Plan A. It's usually Plans B through Z. This is a label you don't want. What do you do when you find out that you are just the rebound?

Suggestion: It shouldn't matter how much you are digging them. You should avoid collaborating with that individual right then and there. How do you avoid being the rebound?

Be cautious. You never know when someone is only inviting you to be with them because at the time, you are the only one available. In situations like this, the smartest thing to do is to go with your gut feeling. I'm not suggesting that if you feel that every time someone asks to spend time with them, you are Plans B through Z. If it was like that, you would be stressed out and you would never go on a date, because you would think that everybody is treating you like the rebound. The best advice I can give you is to play good offense and excellent defense in this game. Grab the rebound, before you become the rebound.

SECRET 3

How Do I Know If Hes Using Me?

You usually don't. You have to keep your eyes open and watch his every move. A lot of men use women for various things—sex, a place to stay, etc. A few days after great sex, your man might ask you for a copy of the keys to your apartment or automobile so that he can get around. Your vehicle makes him look fly and prosperous if it is expensive and up-to-date. Sometimes, even if a man does have a car, he'll take yours just to use and burn your gas.

Men Using You for Sex

A large number of men use women strictly for oral sex and that is it. There are a few telltale ways to find out if he's using you for either oral sex or access to your automobile. He may only come around when he wants one of these two things. After a few months of being with him sexually, he's only taken you out on one or two dates. You only see him when he wants your vehicle or wants you to go down on him. Men also tend to use women who can cook to their liking for a few good meals a couple of times a week. Be very observant of this. Don't let your love get in the way of your intelligence. Sometimes you'll come out ahead just being friends with a man, with no strings attached.

Finally, just because a man is broke doesn't make him a bad person. A lot of people have ups and downs. But after about a week of him just lying around in your bed, eating your food, smoking your weed, drinking your liquor, and not contributing one dime to your household, you should tell him loud and clear to get out. You have a loser on your hands. You need to let him go, especially if he doesn't have a hustle. A man with no type of hustle is a useless man.

It's worse when you have children. It is not fair to your children when they cannot get certain things they need because Mommy is supporting a grown-up child.

SECRET 4

▎ Listen to Your Friends and Family

In certain circumstances, we've been conditioned to not listen to friends or family when they're attempting to give advice or constructive criticism, especially around tricky subjects like a relationship. If your friend or family member doesn't show any interest in your significant other from the beginning, then most likely, they will say anything to separate the two of you.

The majority of the time, they are just waiting to tell you, "I told you so." There is nothing wrong with listening to opinions, both good and bad, but at the end of the day, the final decision rests in your hands. It is you who has to endure the relationship, not other people. Remember, building a relationship is an activity that is going to take time, effort, devotion, and, sometimes hard decisions. Hopefully, experiencing the day-to-day ups and downs of two people being together will provide you with insight and wisdom on how to survive the early stages of building a relationship.

Staying on course with a person, despite the objections from friends and loved ones, shows integrity and commitment, virtues that will take you places in this world. Family and friends should support you in your endeavors, whether they disagree with you or not.

Unfortunately, this is not always the case, so you have to teach them how to support you.

Supplying leadership and guidance around how you want to be treated displays character and self-respect, and will expose and run off those who do not have your best interests at heart.

SECRET 5

Never Pressure a Man into Settling Down

When you do this, it usually backfires on you. After meeting a man, you end up sleeping with him immediately. If you negate the N.P.P.

(no penetration period), the individual that you let penetrate you may think differently. The N.P.P. is a 60 day window period. You got to be strong and try your hardest not to let your guard down.

Do you believe the words "Love at first site?" O.M.D.B. (over my dead body). Those words are a great mythological term. Place yourself in his shoes for a moment. You end up meeting a woman, and she lets you penetrate her area on the very first night. Whether she plays hard to get for the first few hours or not, you still end up having sex.

Now think for a second. Would you take this woman serious? This woman just performed oral sex on you without knowing you, most likely she didn't put a prophylactic on your member before she gave you noggin, (fellatio).

Now answer this? Wouldn't you want to know how many people she let enter her on the first night? How many people she pleased orally during the N.P.P. Wouldn't that be on your mind every time you kissed her? Can you honestly see a future with this woman? I don't think so!

Now let's step back into your shoes. You got to be careful of the things you say when you first start dating someone. Telling a man early that you love him in the relationship is a big no

Telling him that if he's not going to be with you and only you with in the first few dates, that sounds like you're psycho. You just met him a week or two ago. He could be a serial killer, a bisexual, or worse, a sexual predator. Ladies do your research before putting your guard down.

"How do I research someone I just met?" you may ask. Start off by making sure you have his correct name. Most men who are out to play you will give you an alias when they first meet you. To discover the authenticity of the name your new found lover has given you, Google the first and last name. Not only will you find out if you have your friend's true name or not, but you probably will find out additional information about your suitor. Also, encourage your lover to introduce you to his family and friends. Another equally good idea is for you to bring him around your family and friends so that they can help you decide whether or not Mr. Right is right for you. A word of caution when bringing a new male friend around your women: make sure your girlfriends are in solid relationships. All too often, what starts out as a friend innocently introducing her male friend to one of her girls quickly turns to trouble.

Your girl gives your man the eyes, and not just ordinary eyes either, but her bedroom eyes. And we already know what bedroom eyes lead to—the bedroom! Now, when a man sees those bedroom eyes, he sees an opportunity. As soon as he gets the chance to ask your girlfriend for her number, he will. And once she gives it to him, it's on between the two of them.

He starts telling your so-called girlfriend personal things about you, and then she starts to tell him personal things about you. Then the personal things that he tells her, may quickly leak out to your other girls. Things like you can't perform in bed or that your genitals have a funny smell. These nasty rumors get back to you, and now you're enraged and upset. You confront your man. Of course, he denies it. He then tells you your girls are sneaky and warns you to be careful. You believe everything he says, partly to save face and embarrassment, but partly because you've caught feelings for this person. You now sever all ties with your female crew, women who have stuck by you through thick and thin, for a man you don't even really know.

It's a year later now, and after dogging you and your feelings, Mr. Right finally tells you he just wants to be friends. But you don't want to be friends. You are still trying to turn a fantasy relationship into a real one. Loving eyes are blind. Face it: you tried everything to make it work between you and Mr. Right, and you failed miserably. You lost your self-respect and your girlfriends. Cut your losses and move on. Never pressure a man into being with you. The price is too high to pay.

SECRET 6

Is it Smarter to Follow Your Brains or Your Heart?

With all the insanity going on in this world today, not only do you need to follow your heart, you also need to be highly intelligent and perceptive, especially when it comes to those heartbreakers known as the male of the species. With them, you have to be constantly on point 100 percent of the time, because you never know when they're going to pull a stunt.

For example, let's say you are dating a man in the entertainment industry. Every night after work, he's confronted by the most beautiful and sexy women in the industry, who are literally opening up their legs every time they see him.

Before you started dating him, the two of you were friends. You asked him several questions, and he answered them honestly: "Yeah, I sleep with a new woman at least twice a week." You end up dating the guy anyway. After having passionate sex several times, you find yourself really falling for this guy, so you decide to tell him what your feelings are. He responds by telling you he's feeling you too, but he's not yet ready to settle down. As the weeks go by and you realize that you are never going to be number one, jealousy and rage now consume you.

No longer can you tolerate other women being around when you are with him.

Increasingly you begin to monitor his phone calls and curse him out if you suspect he's talking to a woman. During all of this drama you're causing, you unwittingly begin to run your gigolo off.

Now he's left you, and you're all alone, and you can't get over him. So, once again, you followed your heart and not your brains, and now you are all by yourself again. Didn't you learn anything from Tina Turner's "What's Love Got to Do with It?"

Don't fall for anybody but yourself. Keep your sex life and your love life separate. Once you combine the two, you're in trouble.

SECRET 7

What You See Is What You Get

If you see that a man isn't doing anything with himself besides hanging on the corner, getting high, and constantly getting in trouble, then trouble will find you if you choose to involve yourself with that individual. When you encounter a lazy person who just lies around all day, smoking and drinking with no ambitions other than to waste the day away, what makes you think you can change him?

Nowadays, what you see is what you get. It's extremely difficult to change a man for the better, especially if he feels he doesn't have to change. Any suggestions that he should begin to improve himself will offend him and make him angry. When pointing out to someone that his behavior is less than adequate, be prepared for negative responses like anger and accusations of disrespect. These are common defenses from a person who is not interested in improving himself.

If you really are into someone you feel is worth saving from the abyss of nothingness, then you'd better prepare for a long uphill battle.

Some women spend years trying to change a man without success. These women often end up acquiring the same negative habits of their men. During the entire rehab process of Captain

Busta, they denied giving the time of day to any and every man who approached them.

A woman who has her heart set on a man who is unproductive and lazy and doesn't want to change is setting herself up for a long, bumpy ride to nowhere.

SECRET 8

Why Can't Men Take Care of Themselves?

Some men are used to women taking care of them. They view themselves as players, but in reality, they're not. They are men who are incapable of taking on responsibility. In short, they are momma's boys. A momma's boy is someone who has failed to separate himself from his mother emotionally and mentally.

Because some men are, in fact, momma's boys, they never had to do their own laundry, their own cooking, pay their own bills, or make their own bed. Because of this treatment, it's hard for these kinds of men to realize that they are adults now who live in the real world of responsibility.

You should not feel obligated to take care of a man just because you are feeling him. The last thing you need is another child—who is posing as your man—to take care of.

If you really want to build a relationship with this sort of man, make sure he doesn't take advantage of you. Make it profoundly clear in the beginning that you refuse to take any shorts, Make sure that he understands that your kindness is not to be taken for weakness.

Money isn't everything. A man's bank account does not have to be five or six digits either. As long as your man is striving to better him and provide a future for the two of you, you should support and encourage him to the fullest.

Some women only involve themselves in relationships with men who have money. This might be effective and profitable in the short run, but in the long run, they often end up penniless. Everyone goes through their personal ups and downs; it's a part of life. So you need to stick by your man, and he by you, during hard times, especially if you want to experience success. Remember, it was the turtle, not the hare, that won the race. Good things come to people who wait.

The difference between false women and you is that you have integrity. Be very particular about whom you involve yourself with, because your relationships speak a lot about who you are.

SECRET 9

Things Could Change at Any Time

Do your best to be financially independent. No matter how much money your man has, make sure you have some of your own, because you never know when things are going to change. Your man's bank balance could consist of six or seven figures. Suddenly, he hits rock bottom. Three years ago, when he was doing swell, he made you quit your job. As a result, he assumed all financial responsibilities for you and your children.

Now he's broke—and so are you. If you were smart, though, you would have been putting money away for the past three years. It's smart for women today to exercise independence. If a man gets messed up financially, he usually has one or two other women he can live off of until he gets back on his feet.

On the other hand, a woman can't find another man to hold her down unless she's giving up the sex—and then, she's ridiculed for being a jump-off.

People can always change their ways if they're willing. The biggest change is to become financially independent.

SECRET 10

Support Yourself Financially; Do Not Expect Anyone Else To

You are an adult now; therefore you are expected to pay your own way. Paying your own way means getting a job and earning an income. It also means being fiscally responsible, which translates into learning how to budget and save your money.

If you learn and respect the above information, you will never have to depend on a man again. Being financially independent is a wonderful experience, one I encourage you to practice. There are numerous life experiences you are going to encounter that will require you to be financially independent.

For example, let's say you hooked up with a man who has convinced you to move out of state with him. You move to be with him. Everything is going great. Then, all of a sudden, he flips the script on you and begins to beat you. You're frightened and you decide to leave, but you are too many miles from home with no money or job. You are forced to stay with Mr. Abuser and be abused.

Now, had you been financially independent, not only would you have been able to leave, you also wouldn't have been depending on Mr. Abuser.

SECRET 11

Money Matters

When it comes to relationships in our critical and depressing financial times, money matters more than ever. I can only imagine what life is now like for the women who are addicted to high-maintenance living.

Many of the women who are mentally trained to have a man provide for them do not practice independence and may have an emotional breakdown. Why?

This can happen when the man can no longer provide for her needs as she expects. Money is tight, and providers are trying to maintain a budget and still provide for you. The terrible thing is that you are blinded by material things.

All of those extravagant presents your significant other would surprise you with in the past may be out the window now. Your days of spending over $700 on a pair of Jimmy Choo pumps are over.

Unfortunately, your current budget may only be able to afford last season's Coach shoes—on the clearance rack at Marshalls.

Remember that Balmain dress your lover may have surprised you with on Valentine's Day? For that elegant piece of fabric, he dropped over $1,200. Now, you get a $69 dress from H&M.

Welcome to the recession.

Adapting to change may be extremely mind-boggling and uncomfortable. When reality hits, you may find that your man can't just take you to the store each week with his credit card and go on a handbag shopping spree.

Not getting these material things is damaging your relationship, because your lover is using his head when it comes to finances. You start to realize that you are no longer happy.

You find yourself starting unnecessary arguments. You find yourself lying next to your lover with no conversation or sexual contact. Can you believe this? All because he can't provide you with some material things. Now, imagine if you were practicing independence over the years.

If you could purchase those extravagant items for yourself, you would probably be able to save your relationship. As a woman living the average life with a nine-to-five, picture yourself in this situation: You've been in a relationship with a man for more than a year, and your friends and family still tell you that you need to leave that bum alone. You love the guy, but he just seems to be at a standstill. He doesn't want to work. He has no type of hustle. He doesn't cook or clean—but his sex game is magnificent.

When you look at the big picture, you'll come to realize that you're actually supporting a little boy. With your own low-paying jobs, you can barely support yourself and pay your rent. Forget about buying a pair of designer shoes. If there is no improvement in your living situation, how can you help that man out if he doesn't want to help himself? That's when you need to get rid of the sucker.

SECRET 12

Leading a Man On Could Be Hazardous

Believe it or not, some men are more sensitive than women, and leading them on could be a huge mistake. What exactly do you expect to get out of leading a man on anyway? Does playing with someone else's feelings make you feel better about yourself?

How would you like it if someone played with your feelings? You should ask yourself these questions before you start practicing deception. It is not smart to play with another human being's feelings. It's not right, and it can be very dangerous; you never know how a person is going to react when they discover you were just playing a game with them.

They could get physically violent with you. They could hurt you, or worse yet, kill you

(or themselves, making you regret for the rest of your life what you did to them). It's not fair to mislead someone who is pursuing a relationship with you. If you are not feeling a person, tell them straight up that you aren't. If you're into playing with someone's mind and feelings, your wicked ways will come back to haunt you.

So many so-called "players" and "playettes" have ended up penniless because they tried to fleece someone else out of their riches. You have the power to create your own wealth. All you have to do is find your own way to succeed. Once you've earned those treasures, you'll respect your material goods (and yourself) all the more. Earning something is better than tricking someone into buying it for you, especially if you made them believe that you actually had feelings for them.

SECRET 13

Dealing with and Learning from a Man

They say experience is the best teacher, and I agree. There is so much your previous relationships can teach you as you prepare for future relationships. If you suffered in previous relationships because you chose the wrong man, hopefully experience has taught you not to make that mistake again. Nowadays, men tend to play a shrewd and complicated game on women.

The root of their game is the lack of sensitivity and feelings for their prey (you). And it doesn't stop there. As long as you are smiling and going along with their deceitful program, you're all right. But as soon as you put your foot down, they want to respond violently.

On top of that, they refuse to let you go. All of a sudden, they love you. These con artists don't love anyone but themselves. They can't love anything but what you let them get away with. Sometimes it pays just to sit back and observe things so that you can learn to recognize deception when you see it.

Beware of the smooth talkers and the promise-makers. If it sounds too good to be true, then it probably is. If you're clever enough to detect the game in the beginning, cancel the relationship immediately. But if you're in too deep, play along with his game until you can free yourself of the relationship unscathed. Emotionally, a woman can only take so many letdowns and bad breakups. And if you're not careful, sooner or later, you might be the victim of emotional and physical abuse. Think about it!

SECRET 14

Face All Fears

So many women today are afraid to face their fears, especially the fear of losing the person they love. As a result, they tend to let that person run all over them, especially when it comes to infidelity. If you are afraid to approach your man about a serious situation in your relationship, maybe you shouldn't be in the that relationship.

If you are afraid that your man will leave you if you challenge him, then maybe you shouldn't be in that relationship. The two of you are supposed to be able to talk about things that cause trouble in your relationship. You should make sure you talk about things that are bothering you. Never bite your tongue around issues. You have to work to create an atmosphere where you can say what is on your mind, decently and respectfully.

Always remember to be smart, not naive.

One of the biggest issues confronting women today is dealing with an unemployed man. Now, there is nothing wrong with taking care of your man until he gets on his feet, but never support a jobless man indefinitely, especially if he is living with you.

You don't want a grown man depending on you forever; it will only make you miserable and him unproductive. Because you are a leader and you can make it on your own, face all of your fears, no matter what the outcome is. Now I know that may sound harsh and cruel, but when you stand up and face your challenges head-on, you'll be a better and stronger person for it.

SECRET 15

Do not Hold Your Tongue and Put Everything on the Table

This is a very important lesson. At the beginning of any relationship, you should not hold anything back regarding what you are expecting from your partner. If you want to find out certain things about your better half, ask him! Generally, people are not going to volunteer information about themselves that might potentially jeopardize their relationship.

You could be sleeping with a man for a while.

Suddenly, you both let your guard down and enjoy unprotected sex. Two months later, you find out that you are pregnant. A month later, your stomach begins to show there's something cooking in the oven. You decide to tell your man about your pregnancy. After informing him, he disappears and is nowhere to be found for a month. You think you scared him away by telling him so late.

You are now four and a half months pregnant; he calls you and finally apologizes for his absence. He admits to you that he got scared because he did not want his girlfriend that he has been with for three years to find out. You're shocked! You can't believe that the man you thought loved you has another woman.

The very man who planted a seed inside you is heavily involved with someone else? To say you are devastated doesn't even come close to explaining your feelings. Guess what: it's all our fault. You never asked him if he was seeing someone else.

You didn't put everything on the table! Believe it or not, his lady has a big problem now with a pregnant mistress she has never seen before. All because that guy wasn't straight up with you and because you failed to ask the right questions. Always know what you are getting yourself into.

Another example to think about: you have been dating a man for more than a year. What he didn't tell you is that two years prior to meeting you, Mr. Right got arrested for a felony. He didn't tell you because he did not want to run you off (and his attorney assured him he was going to beat the case).

Suddenly, he gets a call from his attorney, informing him that the district attorney has agreed to three years in prison if your man pleads guilty. Simultaneously, his lawyer warns him that if he opts to go to trial and loses, he'll be facing a maximum of fifteen years.

Mr. Right telephones you and tells you, quite abruptly, that he's going to prison next week for three years. He definitely should have told you something, especially after you told him that you loved him two weeks after meeting him. What it all boils down to at the end of the day is that you didn't ask him to put everything on the table from day one.

Demanding to let the chips fall where they may early on in a relationship is best for the relationship. If you remind your partner early (and often) to be honest with you, things will run more smoothly. Honesty is the best policy. Remember, things will always work out for the better if you both continuously communicate about issues, feelings, and decisions.

SECRET 16

Dealing with a Man in Jail

This situation can be very difficult for a woman to handle, especially faithfully. If you truly love the person you are involved with and that person is incarcerated, will you be 100 percent faithful to that person?

That is a good question. But what does "100 percent faithful" mean? Most people think that it means you'll be sexually abstinent throughout the duration of your significant other's incarceration behind the wall— but it doesn't mean that at all.

What "100 percent faithful" does mean is that you will stick by this person's side while they are locked up. This means you will do things like visit them, write them, and send them money so that they'll have things they'll need to get them through the ordeal of prison life.

You'll be surprised how happy you can make someone in prison feel by simply sending them a letter or by taking the time to go see them. Usually, if two people are in a relationship and one of them goes to jail, an arrangement between the two is made. You need to negotiate how you will both handle the new changes in the relationship created by his incarceration.

All sorts of things are possible in a relationship where one individual is in jail. Just because one of you isn't available doesn't mean your needs have to go unmet. I'm not advocating that you cheat on your lover, but I am advocating that you find a way to get what you need.

Among the many things a person needs when their significant other is not available is sex. If you are the kind of person who easily gets sexually frustrated, and masturbation is no longer working for you, then you need to do what is best for you. Again, I'm not advocating unfaithfulness, I'm advocating *satisfaction*. If you do decide to have sex outside of your relationship while your special someone is away, don't fall in love and don't mislead anybody into thinking you're open to having a relationship. Remember, you're committed to a person who's in jail: always remember that.

SECRET 17

Baby Mamas

Having a relationship with a man who has a baby (and the baby's mother) in his life can be challenging. During your relationship, there are going to be times when your man sneaks behind your back and has intercourse with his baby's mother. You may hear rumors and have suspicions about the two of them having sex, but neither of them is going to admit that they are still sleeping together. I'm pretty sure that would eat you up inside.

Look at the situation from a man's perspective. If you were going to visit your child at their baby's mama's house, you would plan to stay there for a couple of hours. If it's at night, you are probably going to stay until the child goes to bed. Once the child is asleep, either you are cajoling her into having sex or she's cajoling you. Either way, you end up having sex outside of your current relationship.

When you go home to your lady after midnight, the first thing she asks you is where you've been. As soon as you say that you've been at your baby's mother's house, an argument ensues. And, of course, you are going to deny any type of sexual activity.

I'm telling you, ladies, involving yourself in a relationship with a man who has a baby with another woman is extremely challenging. Be prepared to hear the following: "Well, that's my baby's mama. What do you expect?"

Anything and everything—including sex—will be associated with the above quote. I guarantee it! And when you think about it, it makes sense; your man is obligated to be in that lady's life, because of the child, forever.

Relax; things are not always as complicated as that. There are situations when a man does not get along with his baby's mama because she is a genuine troublemaker. For example, she may want to go out on a date one night. She asks her baby's daddy to watch the child while she's out. If he says no, she then will make all kinds of threats against him, call you with all types of lies about him, and generally cause havoc for both of you.

Some baby mamas are vicious. They will do anything possible to sabotage your successful relationship. So be mindful of the above before you commit yourself to such a relationship.

SECRET 18

Accepting Children

This lesson is for both men and women. Before you commit yourself to a relationship, you should learn as much as you can about the person, especially if he or she has children.

In that case, as your relationship progresses, you'll want to meet the child or children. Meeting and greeting your significant other's offspring doesn't mean you have to adopt them and play parent to them.

What it does mean, though, is that you're demonstrating a willingness to be a part of their lives. Taking such action also shows character and integrity on your part, and that you are doing all you can to make the relationship work.

In the beginning, the child or children may not immediately accept you in their lives. This is normal for a variety of reasons; just remember that you are the adult and that you have no intentions of being their new parent. As time goes by, this fact will be recognized by the child or children and you will be accepted.

Having children of your own while trying to build a relationship can be troublesome too. Your offspring may disapprove of your significant other. They may feel that their parent isn't paying them as much attention as before. This is why it's always extremely important to make your children feel like they always come first—and they always should come first.

Too many women get caught up in harmful relationships that cause them to lose sight of the fact that their children are their number one priority, not their men.

SECRET 19

What Is Happiness?

Happiness is being in a relationship where you are not the only one who is doing all the loving. You may think you are happy because you believe you have the sexiest guy on the planet and you have all sorts of other juicy things going on in your life. But guess what? That doesn't mean things are all peaches and cream.

Just think about it. If your man is truly sexy, successful, and has big money, don't you think other women will be at him also? So when you find out he's cheating on you, don't get beside yourself. I mean, in your little fantasy world, you may believe you are the only one, but in reality, you're not.

Deep down in your heart, you know there are other women. You know the signs, the excuses, the unexplained absences, the smell of another woman's perfume, etc. In fact, people have been constantly telling you how they've witnessed your man passionately swapping saliva with other women in public. You didn't want to believe it then, and you don't want to believe it now.

Nobody likes to admit they've been played for a fool, and you know your friends are not lying. Besides family and true friends, very few people want to see you happy in a relationship. There are always going to be rumors, but you need to learn to separate rumor from fact. When you hear nasty things about the person you love, give that person a chance to explain him- or herself.

Bring the rumors to your spouse's attention, in a decent and respectful way. This should not be a problem. If it becomes a problem, perhaps there is some truth to the gossip you've been hearing.

When it comes to men and relationships, many men have mistresses. If you were to ask any man currently in a relationship who has a mistress on the side, he will tell you he has more fun with his mistress than with his significant other. The reason why he has more fun and joy with his mistress is because their relationship is carefree with no responsibility or commitment.

I'll also bet you the mistress has already seen you a hundred times—and you don't even know she exists. Why? Because it's all a game to her and your man. People enter into relationships for a variety of reasons, but the central reasons are to be loved and to be happy. Happiness is when your spouse and you are flowing, living in harmony, and loving and trusting each other for real. The idea of an outside romantic relationship by either of you is out of the question. If the two of you were the only two people left on Earth, neither of you would be complaining.

SECRET 20

Do not Be Gullible

Too many women get taken advantage of and fall victim to deceit because they're too trusting. Therefore, I cannot stress enough the importance of being able to quickly recognize game when a man is shooting it at you while trying to manipulate his way into your life.

The most vulnerable types of women are lonely, insecure women. This type of woman is easy prey for male gold diggers, because they want to be loved and accepted. They believe everything a man whispers in their ear.

Mr. Gold Digger knows they don't want to be lonely anymore. He whispers sweet nothings in their ear to lower their guard, making it easy for him to persuade them to do what he wants. And what he wants from these women is to give him their money, credit cards, and whatever else he may desire. To men like Mr. Gold Digger, you are simply a victim, someone to be used for sex, money, or credit, like taking out a car loan for him.

Be particularly careful of men who casually tell you they love you. In fact, a red light should go off in your head when you hear a man you just met tell you that he loves you. Predators will tell you anything to sweep you off of your feet and rock you to sleep.

Another warning sign that you're being played occurs when you are driving with your so-called man. Suddenly, he pulls the car over at an unfamiliar location and tells you to wait in the car. At this point, you should be extremely cautious and aware of your surroundings.

Keep your eyes and ears open. Chances are very strong that your man has stopped by his real woman's house to pay her a quick visit and to put you on display for her. She already knows all about you and who you are.

You see, to them, you're an object of conquest and a meal ticket. Also, by bringing you by his woman's house and putting you on display, he demonstrates his loyalty to her—not you. His real woman has probably done the same thing to men that he is doing to you. Don't be gullible; know who you're with—and why.

SECRET 21

Why Are Men Never Satisfied?

M en have two brains, and the majority of the time, they're thinking with the one between their legs. Most men cannot control their hormones. Please don't let a man get some alcohol in his system, because his libido seems to go off the scale once that happens.

It's not that your man does not love you, ladies; he just does not know how to love you the way you need to be loved. Sadly, ladies, you need to teach your man how to love you—and only you. Teach him that when a pretty face smiles at him, it is not a challenge for him. Some may consider that simple smile to be an invitation to see if he can have sex with the owner of that pretty face and seductive smile. Alas, though, the above behavior and attitude is prevalent among the average male.

The following is a good example of the point I'm trying to make. A woman may see an attractive man and say to herself, "Damn, he's extremely handsome." She may even actively pursue this man, even though she knows this man already has a woman. And once this man—your man—senses this, he's going to blow her back out. It seems that no matter what women do for men, they're simply never satisfied. And ladies, this is nothing to get all stressed out about. *It is not you.*

Remember, some men are selfish and insensitive when it comes to your needs as a woman. Those women who genuinely love their men know what I'm talking about. You have to teach your man how to love you. I repeat this because it is very important in a relationship.

Believe it or not, your man can be a satyr. A good woman with patience and understanding, along with a strong desire to build a passionate relationship with her man, can cure him of this impulse. Now, I am not advocating that you tolerate infidelity or abuse by your man.

All I am doing is identifying what you may be confronted with by the average man out there. Currently, if you are in a relationship that makes you miserable and you feel there is no hope of reconciliation, get out of that relationship right now.

SECRET 22

What You Will not Do for Your Man, Believe Me, Someone Else Will

Ladies, an important thing to remember is that there are thousands of other women out there who are just as beautiful as you or even more beautiful. A great number of these women are willing to penetrate any obstacles that get in their way of assuming your position.

It's the things that may be small in importance to you that will cause your lover to go out there and receive it from the next woman.

Why is it that women get upset when they discover that they are now useless—because Margaret or Sarah accommodated the minor thing that you failed to address?

Does a woman have the right to demand an answer when she asks for the identity of the individual who provided for her significant other when she wouldn't? I'm more than sure that men and women would answer the above questions differently. I think women get upset when they find out that the only reason their man is now satisfied is because another woman stepped in her shoes. This is simply because of selfishness. I say "selfishness" first because what man or woman wouldn't want to keep a smile on his or her lover's face?

It's like, "Hello! Baby, I'm right here.

I'm your woman/man, remember?" Yes, of course all that sounds good and promising, but is it really? A man should not have to step outside of his relationship to be taken care of by someone he is not committed to. By you being selfish, you are blinded by that minor thing that is needed in his life. That minor thing could be larger in his mind than you could ever imagine.

Sometimes you've got to think like a man and figure out what he needs from you: a massage, more affection, or more quality time. Trust and believe me, ladies, but if you can't give a man what he wants at the time he needs it, he'll find it somewhere else.

Of course, women expect their lover not to commit fornication or even lay with the next woman. But when a man's libido is at its peak and you constantly tell him that you are not in a mood for relations, there are only three options: wait until you come around, remain abstinent, or scroll through his iPhone and see if Beatrice or Henrietta can solve his problem. At the end of the day, if option three is his choice, can you blame him?

SECRET 23

Put Yourself in His Shoes

A lot of you ladies tend to think about putting yourself in your man's place. In fact, when you really start to wonder how easy it is for a man to be seduced by a woman, you'll really begin to appreciate fidelity. Right now, as a woman reading this chapter, you are going to put yourself in your boyfriend's, fiancé's, or husband's shoes.

It is a beautiful day outside, and your significant other informs you that he's going to fly to New York City on business. Let's not forget, you're playing the man here. Now, you are in Midtown Manhattan, and you are looking like a celebrity with all your expensive clothes on. You are rocking some Roberto Cavalli jeans, an Ermeneglido Zegna belt, Chopard watch, Brioni suede lace-ups, a Giorgio Armani shirt, and stunner shades.

Every second, women are throwing themselves at you while they are complimenting you on your fly apparel. At the conclusion of your interaction with your new admirer, she discovers that you are only in town for the night. Off of this exchange, you trade numbers. In three hours, you've met four sexy ladies who wanted to see you before you fly back to Boston. You were honest to all of them about your relationship back in the Bean, but they didn't care. All they wanted to do was to get between the sheets with you.

Answer this question honestly: As a man, are you telling me you would not hook up with at least one of those beautiful women without any intercourse going on? In another scenario, you are attracted to one of your girlfriend's best friends. For some reason, she won't stop throwing herself at you.

Are you going to tell your girlfriend? Or are you going to make a move on her? Even better, if she gets you alone and starts passionately undressing you, are you going to say no? Picture that.

SECRET 24

Think! Before Engaging in Unprotected Activity

It seems like men are going to be men until their little things fall off. That being the case, men should study the enormously high rate of sexually transmitted diseases that are prevalent in our society today.

Perhaps if men did pay attention to the danger of sexual diseases, they would not have sex with every woman who shook her ass in front of them. After being enlightened, aware, and alerted to the dangers of unprotected sex, hopefully men will no longer come home to you immediately after having intercourse with the girl next door.

Hopefully, they won't try to make love to you without even taking a bath. And do you know what's worse? The majority of men freely let newly acquainted women wrap their lips around their manhood and not use any protection, as if a sexual disease cannot be transmitted via the mouth.

Uninformed men don't realize that you can easily contract gonorrhea and other STDs through unprotected oral sex, the same way you can catch it through any form of unprotected sex.

When men are unfaithful with loose or promiscuous women, they are not only endangering themselves, they're also endangering the woman they are supposedly in love with. This is a very selfish and dangerous practice. All this can be avoided simply by remaining true to the queen who's been true to you.

SECRET 25

Why Men Cheat

Ladies, when it comes to relationships, there are several universal and essential elements that are necessary for any relationship to form and work: attraction, affection, communication, trust, love, and money.

Attraction is at the core of any relationship. Normally, attraction begins with physical admiration, but it is not limited to appearance alone. Intelligence and wealth have also been known to spark a fire, which can begin to dim for lack of fuel. Other ingredients like affection and compassion are needed.

Let's face it, ladies: there is nothing like being waited on and pampered by that special someone in your life. Affection is about exclusive attention to you and your needs, whatever they are. There is nothing more special than having flowers sent to you out of the blue by your significant other, just to let you know he is thinking of you.

Its lovely when you're special someone takes you out to dinner for no other reason other than to let you know you're loved. It's this type of tender loving care that cements your bond with that special someone and causes the both of you to want to go forward. It also makes you feel like the luckiest person on Earth, too.

Now comes communication. Getting to know each other and build a harmonious relationship can be one of life's best experiences.

Let's get back to the essential element of a good relationship: trust. If you can't trust your man, get rid of him. Ladies, you should not have anybody around that you cannot trust. It's just not smart.

The ultimate tribute a man can pay to a woman is to tell her that he loves her. What is love? A mere statement that makes you feels good? No, love is an activity. Love is discovering all the good things and bad things about a person and learning that your desire to be with that person still exists. Love is sticking by your partner through thick and thin. Love is being honest and forthcoming to your partner about everything if the conditions allow you to. Love, if it's real, will get you through more tough times than money will. And speaking of money …

Just as we cannot survive in this world without money, we cannot survive in our relationships without it either. Whether you are going to dinner, planning your wedding, or simply paying the rent, money is essential.

The most central way to earn money is through gainful employment. I recommend that both parties in a relationship work. There is nothing like financial independence. When both spouses are working in a household, things seem to run smoother than if only one spouse is working. The reasons for this can be many, but from my observations, financial independence connotes self-worth and alleviates the anxiety that can come from worrying about money. But you must be sure that you and your significant other are compatible, because if you aren't, it could hurt you in the future.

Decisions have to be made at this point as to whether you will get serious or not. "Getting serious" means assessing if you share commitment and trust. Many promising relationships have failed in this round because one or both parties were insincere. Despite the passion, hot sex, and wonderful fun that has carried you this far, without trust, commitment, and honesty, the fire is soon going to fizzle out.

Bonding and building for the future come naturally for those who are serious about who they're with. Chasing loose women and cheating is not even up for debate; we don't have the time for such foolishness. We're too busy being responsible and taking care of business.

When a man is in a relationship that is working, for some odd reason, women start to become more flirtatious and interested in him.

But if he's serious about the woman he's with, he'll remain true to her. If he's fronting, he will sleep with every woman he can. It doesn't even have to be your fault, so don't go blaming yourself. It's him, not you. You can be the sexiest woman, your performance in bed could be breathtaking, and you'll still be the victim of an unfaithful man. It all comes down to whether or not your man is true to you.

SECRET 26

Be Open

You have to be open in your relationship. Being open and honest with your mate says a lot about who you are and gives the relationship integrity. If two people in a relationship are open, odds are their relationship is strong and they're happy with one another. Honesty is the conduit to openness.

When a relationship begins to blossom, honesty speeds up the blooming process tremendously. There's something sexy and progressive about how honesty encourages openness between two people who end up with a solid relationship. At the core of their relationship, honesty and openness are found. Of course, being open and honest is risky, but without risk, there is no growth, and without growth, there is no development. Keeping the level of risk low is an easy endeavor. When being honest, expose truths about yourself and your experiences a little bit at a time.

Revealing things about yourself this way allows your mate to absorb things about you slowly. Ladies, contributing financially to your relationship is fine, but don't let yourself get taken for granted. You need to make sure your man is ready, willing, and able to go for his own financial stability, and you must support him every step of the way.

Even if he becomes temporarily unemployed, the beat goes on. The gwop (money) still has to be made. You are a woman and you have needs. It is your man's responsibility to satisfy your needs as long as they're not outrageous. Remember, there is no romance without finance. To be decent and giving in any relationship, being honest and open is the way to go.

SECRET 27

Why Can't Men Be Honest?

The main reason for a man to be dishonest is simple: he doesn't want to lose you. They don't want to see you break down when they tell you they're seeing someone else. Most men are so used to running game on women that when they finally meet a real woman, one they are truly attracted to, it's usually too late to start putting everything on the table.

The reason for this is typically because by this time, they may already be on the fifth fairy tale. The first thing men usually lie about is their name, especially if they've just met a new woman. Obviously they're lying because they're up to no good.

Some men find secrecy a necessity until they're confident a woman can be trusted. In this age of Internet technology, fake names and inaccurate personal information are a must for male gigolos because of search engines like google.

Too much information may expose their fraudulent performance. Also, beware of the secret apartment. It's a secret for a variety of reasons. It's used as a place to bring their promiscuous woman. They may even have another female living there or a gay lover. You never know in these days and times. Finally, when it comes to relationships, lies are told by men especially to impress women.

They feel that by impressing you with lies, they'll not only easily get your attention but your number as well. After several months of bonding, it becomes apparent that it's too late to tell you that he's a paper boy—not a journalist for the newspaper as he first told you.

SECRET 28

What Is True Love?

A lot of you ladies have never found true love. A man will say almost anything he thinks you want to hear, just so he can get into your pants. Great intercourse shouldn't have you telling a man after three days of hot and passionate sex that you love him. And right after telling him you love him, you give him a spare set of keys to your apartment. Are you crazy?

Sex isn't everything. Don't let your guard down simply because someone has whispered some kind words in your ear and sexed you up properly. This person you suddenly claim to be in love with could be a serial killer or have some violent and abusive past that you know nothing about. My point is, you should move slowly in a new relationship.

If it is meant for you and your new mate to be together, the two of you will be together. And if Mr. Right really is Mr. Right, he will take his time too. Remember that relationships need time to work. Very rarely does instant love last.

True love is when you wake up in the morning with your special someone beside you, your eyes meet, and both of you instantly begin to smile from ear to ear.

True love is when you trust your significant other with your life. True love isn't about a man taking you on a $20,000 shopping spree in another state, only to come home after being missing for two days, smelling like some other woman.

It isn't true love when he tries to buy your forgiveness by purchasing you that new car you have been bugging him to buy for the longest time. Don't be so naïve. Money can't buy you love.

True love is when you are into a person because of who that person is, not because of what that person has in the bank. True love is about honesty. It's about looking into your lover's eyes and willingly telling him anything and everything about yourself, no matter what it is.

True love is when you are in love with your best friend. True love is definitely an activity.

SECRET 29

You Don't Need Any Negative Energy around You

I truly hate to see a woman on top of her game and taking care of business saddled with a man who isn't doing a damn thing for himself (or for her). I hate it when he slows her down. This is what I call negative energy, and negative energy is exactly what you do not need in your life.

A man who brings this type of energy to you will adversely affect you emotionally, mentally, and financially. When you start feeling like the man you're with is creating negative energy, leave him immediately.

Often, your best friend or a family member may be able to tell you so-and-so is no good. Perhaps they heard something about the person or see something in them that you don't see. Sometimes they may even want that person for themselves and will put anything in your head so that you will distance yourself from that person. Whatever the circumstance, always make sure your decisions are yours.

SECRET 30

A Love Addiction Is Worse than a Drug Addiction

Some people don't know when to call it quits; enough is enough! If it isn't working even after you've done your best to make it work, cut your losses and move forward. If you are consistently dating men and having intercourse with them after only knowing them for a week or two, something is wrong. If, on top of all this, you're telling them you love them—and they're not telling you they love you back, something is wrong.

If you are searching for Mr. Right, you won't find him this way. What you will find in the end is loneliness and a bad reputation.

Serial dating and screwing will only give you instant gratification. Like all good things, even the thrill of having orgasms and being with a variety of men subsides sooner or later. At some point in our lives, we all have to grow up and be responsible. And in this instance, being responsible is not being taken advantage of by insincere men and their deadly sexually transmitted diseases.

Ladies, keep in mind that while looking for Mr. Right, you must maintain your integrity. This is the twenty-first century! You don't have to sleep around to get a good man. All you will get with this approach is a sexual relationship.

Now, I'm not against sexual relationships if both parties agree to it in their existing relationship. That's fine, but if you're looking for real love, sex is just a component. Remember, real love is an activity that a couple works at.

Don't confuse sex with love. If you do, you run the risk of getting your feelings hurt by a man who will stomp all over your heart. For example, your partner might sleep in bed with you three nights in a row and then you might not see him for a week. When you do see him, you ask him where he has been for the past week. He tells you, in no uncertain terms, to mind your own business. With this blunt response, you want to argue! But you're not his girlfriend or his boss; he does not have to report to you. In fact, he decides that you're asking too many questions and walks out on you.

Now you're hurt and angry, and moreover, you blame yourself that he left. So you decide to call him and beg him to come back—and he never does. A few weeks later, through the grapevine, he discovers that you are telling all of your girlfriends that he is your man.

SECRET 31

Do Not Let Men Walk All Over Your Heart

Some women let men get away with breaking their hearts after they've invested some time in a man. These women have a tendency to think out loud. "He's going to change. I know he loves me. He won't do it again. I don't believe that rumor. My best friend would never sleep with my man. I've known her since high school."

Never put anything past a man. Men have a smooth way of making women believe in them. It's called *game*. Nearly all men have game (as do women). A man with an A game can make an unsuspecting woman believe almost anything.

Say a man cheats on you with your best friend or your favorite cousin, or you spot him driving by with another lady in your car when he's supposed to be somewhere else, taking care of business. After you witnessed this, just to add insult to injury, he'll have the audacity to deny everything. After you've forgiven him yet again, you'll be cooking for him, ironing his expensive jeans—the ones you bought, just so he can go out and spend some money and quality time with the next female who's ready and willing.

On top of all of this, you pleased him orally so that you could defuse the argument the two of you were having because you accused him of cheating on you. Now, after a week of trying your hardest to give him the cold shoulder, everything is back to normal again. Or so you think.

Lo and behold, the very next night, he stays out all night and doesn't even call.

Sound familiar? It's called walking all over your heart.

SECRET 32

A Good Orgasm Only Temporarily Allows You to Forget All the Pain He Has Caused You

There's nothing like good sex and a cigarette after having a huge fight. Sound familiar? Whether the fight started over him cheating on you or simply not spending enough time with you is unimportant at this point. What is important, however, is how Mr. Smooth manipulates your life and you. You couldn't even leave Mr. Smooth if you wanted to, could you? He has you wrapped around his finger!

Some guys have that kind of charisma. Thanks to their good looks and inviting smiles, women like you melt at the sight of them.

Unfortunately for you, you have one of those types of guys. You know the kind of guy who has that look, the one that makes your hormones go wild. Admittedly, you may be able to dodge him for a week or two when you're angry, but when he catches up with you, it's a wrap.

Game over. You melt like ice in hell. The grudge you were holding is gone, and Mr. Smooth is now leading to your bedroom to finish you off sexually. You've now released all the anger, rage, and frustration you had toward Mr. Smooth by way of a volcanic orgasm. Mr. Smooth rolls off of you and sits on the edge of the bed and lights a cigarette while you stare at the ceiling, legs still wide open, wondering why you were angry at him in the first place. He's conquered you once again. All your intentions of moving onward and upward are gone.

Having intercourse with Mr. Smooth didn't do anything but make things worse. Instead of thinking with your head, you let your swanson (vagina) do the thinking. Now you are back to square one. Mr. Smooth and his johnson between his legs are calling the shots, as usual. The next time Mr. Smooth and you run amuck (and there will be a next time), follow your brain instead of your hormones.

SECRET 33

Cry on Paper, Not in Public

It's not only embarrassing to cry in public, it's unladylike to shed tears over a man who doesn't feel the same way about you as you do about him. It's a shame how easily men will mislead women.

Don't get me wrong: there's nothing wrong with crying at all. We're all human. It is just not smart to be crying over somebody who has been consistently unfaithful to you. And do you know what is really crazy? He's probably sitting beside you on your bed right now, telling you how much he loves you. And you're probably eating up everything he's telling you. What you really should be doing is telling his sorry ass to pack his shit and get the hell out. That's what you should be doing.

Now, how are you feeling? Good, right? If you need to release some additional energy after tearing that man a new asshole, go out and enjoy yourself, alone or with a real friend (male or female) who truly loves you.

Approaching your man with an issue in a sensible and respectful manner will almost always force him to respond to you honestly because you are not pressuring him into a situation that is uncomfortable. By being forthcoming and honest, you're bound to obtain favorable results while not losing any respect for yourself in the process.

SECRET 34

Band-Aids Can't Heal You

"Band-Aids can't heal you" is a powerful statement. When you hear this statement, your brain should begin to scramble. I can picture you sitting down, thinking to yourself, *Damn, what exactly does that mean?*

The scariest thought is that you might consider mutilating or hurting yourself because of a bad relationship. When a woman thinks about hurting herself, cutting her wrist, or harming her significant other, she's crazy. After all the drama of the emergency room thing, the police thing, and the courtroom thing, you'll still be hurting. Revenge isn't the correct way to get even.

You ask, "What will heal me then?" Time and patience. Sometimes it is good to be alone so that your wounds will have time to heal. Waiting for the right individual to come along may take time, so be prepared to take a long respite from men. Use this free time to talk to other women who are going through the same kinds of things you are. It's also okay to have a male friend to talk to, as long as he doesn't try to sleep with you.

SECRET 35

Payback: Things You Just Do Not Do

Beware of doing things that you'll end up regretting when you try to get even with your man or your ex-man. For example, you may have found out that he's cheating on you. Maybe you feel feeble because of the way he left you hanging. Whatever the case is, do not sleep with one of his friends (or his enemies), because at the end of the day, those kinds of behaviors just make you look bad. And honestly, the only person you end up hurting is yourself. This sort of thing can also damage your reputation as a bona fide lady.

Going through his cell phone and phoning every woman's number in it may seem like a good thing to do, but doing this and making up all kinds of insane rumors about your relationship with him is extremely immature. When you engage in this type of activity, you run the risk of damaging valuable business relationships for you and your man.

We all love to repay someone in kind who has done us harm or has disrespected us in some way. It's always better to just cut an individual like that out of your life totally. Slashing their tires and smashing their car windows isn't doing anything but causing more problems. You should simply give people who are mistreating you the cold shoulder.

SECRET 36

Should I Go Through a Man's Pockets?

This is a big no-no! If you are in a relationship, you and your significant other are supposed to trust one another. Going through his pockets means there is no trust. If there is no trust, there is no relationship. How can you sleep with a man and think about wicked ways to hurt him? That type of thinking is unhealthy and harmful to both him and you.

What are you looking for when you are searching through your man's pockets? Money? Evidence of another woman? This sort of activity is a proof that your relationship is already in trouble, regardless of the presence of another woman. And what if you do find evidence of another woman? What are you going to do?

Asking him about her may conceivably start an argument, and that can lead to a lot of yelling and screaming and maybe even violence. You may also get the answers you seek—answers you may not want to hear, like she's better in bed than you. This response will be painful to hear, I'm sure.

Therefore, to avoid any of the above ugly scenarios, sit down with your man and try to work things out. Get support from a friend or relative if you need to.

SECRET 37

Some Men Just Don't Have What You Need

Have you ever asked yourself what it is you are looking for in a man? What are some of the things you need from a man? Well, now is the perfect time to ask yourself these questions. Take time to think carefully about what was missing in your past relationships— communication, trust, sex, etc. Don't dwell on just the negative things; think about all the good things as well. Once you discover what those things are, keep a mental note of them, because they'll be extremely helpful to you in your next relationship.

These days, you just can't climb in a relationship not knowing what you want or need. The world is just too complicated. Moreover, you should always know (or at least have an idea about) what it is you want out of life. Knowing this gives you direction and allows you to travel great distances in your relationships and in life. You're more likely to be successful too.

So if you want to keep that pretty smile on your face at the end of the day, know what it is you're after and go for it. Disappointments will come and go—they're part of the game— but if you know what you want for yourself, you and your smile are consistent.

SECRET 38

Are You Sick of Wearing Sunglasses?

I'm not talking about the designer shades you're wearing to match your $3,000 handbag. "Then what exactly are you talking about?" you say to yourself. What I'm trying to say is, "Aren't you tired of getting so abused physically that you have to try to cover up those black eyes with a pair of Betsy Johnson shades?" Don't you know it's not cool to let yourself suffer from abuse? How can you stay with someone who beats the breaks off of you constantly, and then tells you that he is sorry and that he loves you?

There are too many men out there to be stuck with one who cannot express himself without putting his hands on you. He doesn't do anything for you but give you good sex. But is the price you are paying for that sex worth the beatings? That is the question you should be asking yourself. Are you being abused right now? Are you confused? Do you not know how to get help?

There are a few ways to get yourself out of this crazy situation you're in. One sure way is to leave, and if he won't let you leave, call the police. Another way is to get couples' counseling. If Sluggo refuses to attend counseling with you, that should be a red flag. It's time for you to leave.

If you look at the bigger picture, you should be able to see that any man who beats you is incapable of loving you. The only thing he loves is beating you.

SECRET 39

Ask Yourself Whose More Important

Don't ever put a man before you or your children. I promise that you'll regret it—and your children will hate you for doing it. Imagine what is going through the minds of your children when they realize that a complete stranger gets more of your attention, care, and love than they do. Children have feelings and long memories; they're sensitive too. They require your undivided attention.

Do you honestly think a man would put you before himself or his family? Please, don't be naive! They're too into themselves for them not to come first. It's not difficult for a man to act like you are the most important person in the world to him; it's all game. Seeing women fall victim to this charade makes me sick to my stomach. How can you give up so much of yourself to a person who refuses to show you any affection or attention in public?

When it comes to men, you really need to be as clever as they are. You need to get into the habit of asking yourself one very important question: "Would he do for me as I am doing for him?" If you don't like the answer, then some things in your relationship either need to improve or change completely, because you are getting the short end of the deal.

SECRET 40

How to End an Unhealthy Relationship

You definitely have the right to be frightened. We've all heard the horror stories around men who seriously injure their spouses and, in some extreme cases, kill them. If you feel threatened, intimidated, or afraid because of violence in your life, you need to put this book right down and get out now.

Nobody has the right to put their hands on you. Once you have removed yourself from that harmful situation, assess whether or not you want to salvage the relationship. If you decide to rebuild your relationship with your man, he has to agree to follow your leadership as to how you want to be treated in the future. And, as I have stated earlier, make sure couples' counseling is included in the rebuilding process of your new relationship.

Now, let's say because of machismo or downright ignorance, your man refuses to participate in the rebirth of the relationship. He wants to continue the status quo of beating on you whenever he chooses. At this point, you have no choice but to proceed to the local courthouse to get a restraining order against this criminal who has been using you for a punching bag.

Sometimes women want to involve their brothers and other family members. Many times, this only leads to bigger problems. If someone else gets hurt defending you, this can lead to an ongoing war.

Sometimes, changing your phone number and moving many miles away from him works.

If you don't have any friends or family support, get online and find a local shelter to check into, just until you can get on your feet. Whatever you do, don't let the abuse continue. Please do not let your children endure the horror of seeing their mother being abused.

SECRET 41

Doing the Same Thing Only Brings the Same Results

In other words, if you continue to do the same old harmful stuff, you'll get the same old results. If you choose to return to the same man who has hurt and abused you, you'll end up hurt and abused again.

Likewise, if you involve yourself with a man who sells drugs or a man who is heavily involved in street activity, nothing good will come out of the relationship. If you deal with criminals who refuse to change their lives around, I guarantee you that they will either end up in jail or dead. Either way, you end up alone or hurt.

The problem with the above relationship is that feelings got in the way of intelligent thinking. Falling in love with thugs, drug dealers, and gang bangers is profoundly risky. At some point, the negative activity of breaking the law will come to an end, and where will your relationship be after that? These are the kinds of questions you need to be asking yourself.

SECRET 42

Is Breaking Up a Hard Thing to Do?

A lot of women are stuck in relationships they truly don't want to be in. Whether it is fear of being alone or that they simply don't want to hurt anybody's feelings, they endure misery with a smile on their face. And if you ask them about their choice to stay, most woman in this situation will have a good excuse (in their minds, at least) as to why they don't leave.

First of all, if the thrill is gone and the fire is out, you need to leave. Leaving isn't always a bad thing. On the contrary, it can be a good experience for both of you. You don't always have to depart on bad terms; you can remain friends and support each other in finding and developing new relationships.

Most relationships end abruptly without consideration or support of those involved. No wonder nasty and violent breakups occur. What do you expect when feelings are involved? Breakups need to be planned delicately so that both parties are involved in the dynamics of separating.

If you've been attached to someone for a long period of time, letting go can be a difficult and painful process. Decency and empathy, if possible, should rule the day. Most men will do the honorable thing by accommodating you once you decided irreconcilable differences cannot be worked out. You'll know when you've had enough and it's time to move on; you'll feel it in your heart.

SECRET 43

Dealing with Stress at Work

The workplace is definitely *not* the place to be getting migraines or teary-eyed over a man. Your place of work is your place of work; it's not an environment for you to dump your personal problems. Never bring your personal problems to work if you can help it. When you bring your personal life to work, you're making your business show business, and that's not cool.

You are effectively giving your co-workers a green light to be nosey and to ask all sorts of stupid questions you may not want to answer. Staying home from work because of a man is also a huge mistake. Life goes on after any breakup, and your work is your livelihood. The only people who should interfere with your livelihood are children and family members.

Now, if you have to take a day or two off to regroup from a breakup, that's understandable; but after that, try your best to keep your personal problems at home. Your job is your most important means of earning a living, and no one should interfere with that.

SECRET 44

How to Overcome a Bad Breakup

Congratulations! You finally broke out of that abusive relationship that was causing you so much pain and embarrassment. So why are you continuously crying every day? You are not eating or sleeping, and you've lost a lot of weight. Your family and friends are beginning to worry about you.

It's time to move on and stop dwelling on the past. I understand that you invested a lot in a relationship that didn't go anywhere, but it's not the end of the world. For every ending, there is a new beginning! A better man will come along, but until he does, you need to heal yourself, both emotionally and physically. Take time out to be good to yourself.

Go get a massage, pedicure, and manicure. After that, try going to the gym to get a good sweat. Working out helps to relieve stress and tension. Water does too. A good swim or an hour in a hot tub or sauna will do wonders for you. Whatever you choose to do, make sure you do it. Put your phone on voicemail and go have some fun.

Speaking of phones, when you return from your weekend hiatus, it'll be smart of you to change your phone number. It is time to rid yourself totally of all negative energy associated with your past relationship. What's also therapeutic is reading a good novel. If you enjoy reading, try reading something you've never read before. I know the perfect novel for a woman to read; it's called, *I Love You Doesn't Mean Shit,* written by yours truly, Surpaul Cottrell. I'm not going to share any of the details now, but at the end of this book, I have included an excerpt of the novel. It is definitely a must-read.

It has probably been a few days or weeks since you have slept with a man. At this point, you can be extremely vulnerable. Don't backtrack, and don't call your ex for any reason. Now, understandably, your libido is off the charts and you want to hit the clubs. If you do, do not leave the club with just any Bob, Hank, or Henry. Be patient, and preserve your goods (and your swanson) for Mr. Right. You'll feel it in your gut when he appears. But until he does, enjoy the single life and focus on you.

SECRET 45

Take It One Day at a Time

After breaking up with your man, things can be tough for a while. Take a few days to heal and regroup, but don't take forever. The longer you take to get past a breakup, the longer it will be before you are again on the road to success. For every ending, there is a new beginning, and this is what you are now about. Get rid of the old and meet the new.

There is no need to go out searching, either; let the new come to you. Your job is to be prepared for Mr. Right. While you are waiting, be good to yourself. Get your hair, nails, and toenails done. Do some shopping downtown and feel good about being *you*.

Women seem to think they have to be in a relationship to be validated. On the contrary, you validate the relationship. While it is true that you contribute half of a relationship, your half is an important half. Without you, there would be no sunshine, no sexual relief, and no inner development of maturity, the things that only come with building a real relationship with a real woman. So take your ex off of your mind and prepare yourself for good things to come.

SECRET 46

Include Yoga in Your Life

Many times after breaking up with someone significant in our lives, we find ourselves seeking support and comfort from others. Rarely do we look inside ourselves for our inner strength. An excellent way to discover the riches and power that the self-possesses is through yoga.

Yoga is a combination of physical and spiritual exercises that strengthen the mind and body. Through poses and stretches, yoga increases and develops flexibility throughout the body. This ultimately sharpens the mind, which allows you to exercise sound judgment.

The spiritual half of yoga teaches you how to breathe properly through meditation. Meditation connects you with your inner self and awakens you to who you really are and to all the strengths you truly possess.

Once the physical is balanced with the spiritual, you will be at peace with yourself. When you are at peace with yourself, you become sure of yourself. You stand strong.

Being able to stand strong gives you the power to withstand the enormous challenges the modern woman encounters on a daily basis.

Yoga may not work for everyone who tries it. For example, you may dislike the meditation aspect of yoga but enjoy all the stretches and exercises it offers. In any event, I encourage you to take a few moments out of your schedule to experiment with some different ways to relieve stress—and feel good about yourself doing it.

SECRET 47

There is Nothing Wrong with Change

Change can be extremely developmental and powerfully beneficial to those courageous enough to embrace it. When your best thinking lets you down, you may need to change the way you think. There is nothing wrong with changing your mind, especially when you feel that failure is on the horizon.

Nobody likes to fail, and nobody has to. Most often, we fail because we are afraid to change and explore the new and unknown. This is especially true in relationships. The first few months can be going fine—and then all of a sudden, you realize the relationship isn't going anywhere. You tried everything that you could possibly do to make things better, but nothing is working. This is the time when you need to change your relationship. It has run its course.

Men are like jeans inside a Neiman Marcus store. You take one pair at a time and try them on in a dressing room. After wearing them and walking around in them for a while, you may decide to buy them so you can keep wearing them. You may decide that you need a new pair.

My point is that your decision to keep the jeans depends on how comfortable they are. You like them because of how they make you feel or how good they make you look when you are wearing them. Being in a relationship is similar; if the relationship satisfies you, you'll stay. If it doesn't, you'll leave. Makes sense, right? Save your money so you can secure a safe place to stay. If you have children, plan for them accordingly as well.

When children are involved, breakups can be more difficult, especially if they're attached to your significant other. Sometimes children experience extreme difficulties around parental breakups, particularly when favorable relationships exist between them and their parents. Often, the end of these relationships can be very difficult to navigate. If there is another man involved, it can take children some time to adjust to a new man.

Children can be clueless as to what is going on in the lives of adults. Therefore, when you are single and looking for Mr. Right again, do not bring a new man around your children too quickly. The process of introducing your child or children to your new man is a delicate one that you should ease in to. Don't rush it!

SECRET 48

Practice Being Patient

Everybody talks about Mr. Perfect. Some women get tired of everyone else talking about how they found Mr. Perfect, so much so that they become stressed out—and become a serial dater. Sometimes you have to travel the world (or the states, depending on how financially stable you are) to find Mr. Perfect. Some women are fortunate enough to have only traveled as far as the local bar.

When looking for Mr. Perfect, try switching locations. Remember that variety is the spice of life. Depending on what type of man you're looking for, a jazz club or a low-key but upbeat cafe might be the spot also.

Whatever path you decide to take, always exercise patience. Some people do not know how to be patient, while other people live their entire lives exercising patience and caution. If you don't have patience, learn patience today and you'll never regret it. Rushing into relationships is dangerous because good sense and judgment are often pushed to the back burner.

Impatience almost always puts women in precarious situations when playing the dating game. You run the risk of being perceived as easy, desperate, and vulnerable. In order to avoid these pitfalls, take your time, study your prey, watch for his weakness—and then exploit it to your benefit.

In short, always maintain the upper hand when meeting somebody new. Read your prey first before rushing in to subdue him. Initially, make sure the two of you have something in common, such as similar taste in movies, music, or sports. Maybe it's reading a good novel or playing chess. Whatever it is, make sure you both enjoy the activity.

Try creating a test or standard that Mr. Perfect must pass to get with you. He doesn't need to know he's being tested, but he does need to know that you don't have time for any games. Let him know that you will cancel him as quickly as a two-minute brother climax.

SECRET 49

Starting All Over Again

Rebuilding your life can be a difficult process, especially if you have devoted years of your life to creating a particular type of relationship you thought would make you happy forever. Sadly, you learned the hard way that the majority of relationships you were involved in were not for you. Lucky for you, though, it's never too late to change.

Starting over again really isn't as bad as you think. For every ending, there is a new beginning. Breaking up after five years of sheer madness is easier than enduring an additional ten years of sheer madness.

Many women are reluctant to start over again because they fear the unknown. They would rather deal with the devil they know. The problem with this is that they continue to suffer and be miserable. How can you conclude that something major in your life is wrong and not want to correct it? To stand by and be miserable is not intelligent. Miserable people end up doing crazy things like becoming alcoholics or drug addicts—and that just isn't cool.

After you've realized you are no longer happy in your current relationship, make plans. If for whatever reason, you are unable to immediately sever ties, take your time and plan an exit strategy.

SECRET 50

I Love You Doesn't Mean Shit

L ove is an activity, not just a kind statement of intent, affection,
or admiration. It is a day-to-day performance of being giving,
decent, and real by two people who share an attraction for one another.

Love also means standing by the person you love, no matter
what, and keeping it 100 percent real with that person. It also
means thinking and talking positively about the person you love.
When you are a million miles apart from the individual you love,
if the first thing you think about when you get up in the morning
is that person, that's love.

Love means that if things are not going right between the
two of you, your differences bring you closer instead of pushing
you farther apart. Love means having a real and true friend you
can trust when everyone else seems to turn against you.

Love is not a bunch of empty promises made by somebody
who doesn't even know what the word itself means. To simply *say*
"I love you" doesn't mean shit.

Don't forget to follow @Cottrell_vision & @immahbeastwitit
on
all Social Media Platforms

SNEAK PREVIEW

"I LOVE YOU"
DOESN'T
MEAN SHIT

CHAPTER 1

(ANESSA-WOO SPEAKS)

Growing up in the city of Boston, I had always been infatuated with the fall of snow. There's nothing like living in a loft on Newbury Street, inhaling some exotic smoke from your bong while enjoying the scenery. The section of Boston I lived in was known as Copley Square. Copley Square is the area where there's people who like to spend money on European jeans, fabrics, and shoes. I love shopping on Newbury Street after I have some smoke in my system.

When I was twenty-two, my father was murdered in the streets of Dorchester. He was a retired heroin dealer. When he gave up the game, his partner got hooked on heroin. Two years after my father stopped hustling, his ex-accomplice hit rock bottom. My father tried to help him out plenty of times by trying to place him in different detox centers.

Then one day he came to the house and threw a gun to my father's head. He told him that he wanted a million dollars or his life. My father told him, "Over my dead body." I witnessed a bullet go through the back of my father's head. I was left with blood on my face and my clothes. As I screamed, he aimed the firearm at me. But then he decided to place it in his mouth instead—and I watched him blow his brains out on the wall. For a little over a year, flashbacks played in my head every day.

I turned to smoking pot as the months went by. Alex, my best friend at Boston University, was there for me throughout the tragedy. He was a Caucasian who was attracted to the same sex and was very open about it. Everyone started to call him "Gay Alex." That name has stuck with him ever since. I became a pot head because of him.

There's nothing wrong with smoking some good weed. I'm very focused, plus I have a great job. I'm a registered nurse at Boston City

Hospital. I have a snow-white BMW pay my bills, and have enough to live a situated life. My father left behind a lot of money, plus the lovely loft that I now own. My father was full-blooded Dominican. My mother was 100 percent Vietnamese. I was given her last name when I was born. When I was a little girl, my father ended up getting custody of me. I haven't heard anything about my mom since then.

I have to open the door; I believe that's Gay Alex ringing the bell. I looked out the window instead, and when I saw that it was him, I buzzed his happy ass in. I wanted to get in the shower, so I decided to leave the front door cracked for him.

I entered the bathroom garmentless as the chilly temperature attacked my body. I left the bathroom door halfway cracked as I threw my aching body in the water. My muscles were very sore from going extra hard in the gym last night. I started following @ Immahbeast on Instagram. There are many challenges on his page. Plus I lost 12 pounds in two weeks doing #thecottrellmethod. I was banging out some squats last night. My ass and legs were killing me! I took a long bath last night to soothe my body, but when I woke up, I could feel the ripping of my muscles. I thought that the smartest thing to do would be to get in the tub and let the steamy water smash against the ripped tissue in my body.

Twenty minutes later, I climbed out the shower and dried off my entire body. I wrapped the towel around me and I exited the bathroom.

"What's up, Alex? What are you breaking up over there?" "A little bit of orange crush." "So it's 'orange crush' now? Every week you come over here with a new name for weed."

"I don't make it up, girl; that's just the name my guy gives me." I walked into my bedroom to throw some cucumber body lotion all over my body. I threw on a simple under garment set and a pair of jeans on my ass. I walked into the living room and threw myself on the soft couch next to Alex. "Girl, throw a shirt on. I don't need that flesh in my face," Alex stated. "Relax. I can't walk around my loft wearing a bra? You're acting like you haven't seen me nude over a dozen times." "Anessa, I'm just joking. Calm down. Here, I just stuffed the bowl for you." Alex handed me a lighter as I put the fire on the orange crush, and put my moist lips on the mouthpiece of the bong. I inhaled smoothly, letting the smoke attack my lungs. I started to cough wildly. Alex couldn't stop laughing. I pulled myself up from the couch and

I then took off running to the kitchen to crack open a bottle of water. That third pull went straight to my brain.

That was definitely some grade-A smoke. I grabbed Alex a bottle of water and then walked back into the living room.

"Damn, girl, you can't handle the smoke," Alex said. "It went down the wrong pipe, you jerk."

"Is that so? Oh yeah, I forgot to tell you about last night." Alex said.

"What happened last night? "Well, I met this guy online. We've been chatting on messenger for a few days now. I invited him over to my place last night. I'm not gonna lie; it only took five minutes for us to get down to business. When I tell you that this guy was only like six inches and couldn't work it, girl, I was ready to throw him off the balcony. I hopped in the shower quickly and got dressed. When I came back to the bedroom, this nympho had the audacity to be flipping through the channels, lying naked on my pillow with a soft prick. I told him that it was time for him to go and that I had things to do."

"So what did he say?" I replied. "He said, 'You can't be serious. I only have been here for twenty minutes.' I said, 'Exactly.' I guess he thought that he was putting in work. I kept calling you to help me get this freak out of my spot. You kept ignoring my phone calls."

"I was in the gym last night for two hours. I'm sorry. So, how did you get him out?"

"I told him that I didn't want to call the cops, but I would if I have to. He was a lot bigger than me, so I was a tad bit petrified. He finally got dressed. He asked me if I was going to drive him home. I told him that I couldn't. He told me that he's too classy to be taking the bus. Then he asked me to pay for his Uber. He said that he lived all the way in Woburn. Now I was starting to feel like I was paying a whore to horse me. I got real upset. I told him it sounds like a personal problem. I raised my voice at him and realized he was big for nothing. He said that he had no money and he was broke."

"How did he get to your house?"

"I picked him up from the Boston Common," Gay Alex said. "I took him to this gay bar on Kneeland Street. We had a few drinks then

I took him back to my place. I was devastated when I realized that I gave up my goods to a broke maniac. I wish I had cash to give him, but

I only had my black card on me. If I had it, I still would've had regretted giving it to him. I don't pay to get my back blown out. Mothafuckers need to pay me."

"You're crazy. So what happened? Tell me the rest of the story."

"He finally left the house. I wanted to make sure that he was completely out of my building, so the both of us walked downstairs.

He told me that he couldn't believe that I was going to leave him out in the snow alone. I completely ignored him. I walked to my parking space and unlocked the doors with the device on my keychain. As soon as I pulled the handle on my door, I hit the automatic lock button, then climbed in my car. I turned my car on and turned my wipers on to take the snow away from the windshield. This psycho bastard was standing there looking into my eyes. I felt like I was filming a scene in a movie, and I was the victim getting chased by Michael Myers. All I was thinking of was that damn melody that they play when he's about to kill somebody.

"I backed up my car until I bumped into the bumper of the car behind me, "Alex continued. "I noticed that I had enough room to pull out of the spot and not smash into him. I was surprised that he let me pull out of the spot. I thought that he was going to jump in front of the car. When I pulled off, I looked into the rearview mirror, and there was a big gay guy running a few feet behind my car. He ran until I ran through a red light, almost smashing my Corvette. That was the craziest thing I had ever experienced. I went straight to Damien's house, and we did it all night!"

"Damien's going to leave you one day if you keep cheating on him," I said. "I know, but I can't help it. Plus he would never find out. Well, that was my story. Are we still going to that sex-toy party at the The HighBar?"

"Of course we are. I need a new gadget. I'm tired of using my fingers."

"Is that so?"

Throughout his entire story, both of us kept hitting the bong as he continued to stuff the bowl two more times. I was high as hell.

I walked back into my room and continued to get dressed. I knew exactly what I wanted to wear, and twenty minutes later, we got into my car and headed to the party.

CHAPTER 2

(SEAN SPEAKS)

It only gets better. It can't get any worse.

That's what I tell myself when I think about that trifling ex-girlfriend of mine. I went through so much bread messing with her. Every day, she's telling me that she loves me; then we finally bought a two-family crib together. Then I hook her up with a real estate agent who was a good friend of my family to help us refinance the crib.

This chick tells me she is falling out of love with me.

Two days later, she kicks me out the crib and we break up. A week later, she's going out with his ass. *"I love you"* doesn't mean shit, I guess. She had the audacity to tell me that I had to continue to pay my portion of the mortgage. I thought that shawty was messing with that dawg food, talking stupid like that. The crib was under her name. I didn't mess up; she did. Her boyfriend could spend bread on the mortgage. *Well, shit happens,* I thought. I learned to move on. That chick left me over a year ago.

Now I'm touring overseas with six digits in my bank account legally. I know she hears my songs on the radio. She probably wants me back, but I will never take a step back. I'm glad that I lucked out messing with Craigslist. I was searching for a little spot to lay low at, around the Copley Square area in Boston. Three days ago, I went to check out a spot. Now I'm back here with a U-Haul filled with mostly clothes. I got two cool-ass white boys who are studying at Fisher College to room with me. Our rent is $3,000 a month, and the apartment was well worth it. The spot was huge. I didn't mind spending a stack to live across the street from Copley Mall. My best friend Big rented the truck for me and decided to help me move into my new apartment. I'm glad that it had stopped snowing.

After moving shit for an hour, we finally finished. Big helped me set up my king-sized bed. It took about two hours to set up everything in my room. Big didn't get a chance to meet my new roommates. When they let me in the crib, they went to the hardware store to make me a copy of the keys to the apartment. While we were moving, they must've walked right by Big. And now, they're back, walking into the apartment now. I headed to the living room as Big followed me.

"What's up, fellas? I wanna introduce you to my main dude. We call him Big."

"Big! Big like Biggie Smalls? That's cool, man.

My name is Cornelius. Nice to meet you, Big."

"What's up, Cornelius?" Big said.

"They call me Zachery. Hey, do any of you brothers smoke pot?

I was just wondering. After moving all this stuff, I was thinking that maybe you guys wanted to try some of this AK-47."

"AK-47, what's that? Like some awesome kindbud mixed with some dawg food," Big replied.

"Yeah, we both smoke. That sounds like something that will get us in that world I would love to be in right now."

Big is crazy, I think. *These white boys are gonna think he's nuts.*

"Trust me, you brothers will love it," Zachery said. We followed Zachery to the other side of the living room, where we had a bong set up on the large coffee table. I never in my life blew trees out of a bong before. The thought of it just made me feel like a rock blower. I wonder if Big was thinking the same thing I was thinking. These two geeky-looking students definitely had the living room looking like something on *MTV Cribs*. They had two big-ass flat-screens beside one another with a fireplace right beneath them. They had a leather sectional that seemed to be custom-made; it went around the walls of the entire living room. "You brothers have a pretty nice set-up here," Big said sarcastically.

Thanks. So Big, what do you do? Sean's an singer. Do you got lyrics too, or are you just his hype man?" Cornelius asked.

"No, brotha! I'm not a rapper or a hype man. I own real estate."

"What type of real estate?"

"I buy houses and convert them into condominiums." "That's cool, man. That's a smart idea," Zachery said. Cornelius torched the bong and then began to pass it around the cipher.

"So what do you guys do?" Big asked.

"Well, I go to Fisher College for computer programming. All I do is download free stuff, create websites, and hack other people's computers all day," Cornelius said.

"What about you?" Big asked Zachery.

"I go to Fisher too. I'm going there for business management and marketing."

"That's cool."

I definitely got some cool roommates with some good smoke.

I'm glad that my dude Big helped me settle into my new spot. I never thought that I would have a roommate or two. I got tired of wasting gwop on hotels just to smash suttin' new. Of course, I had the key to a few different birdys' cribs, but I needed my own spot that they didn't know about.

CHAPTER 3

(ANESSA-WOO SPEAKS)

What a night last night. I definitely had a great time with Alex. I can't believe that I'm at work this morning still feeling nice. I'm about to kick it with my girlfriend Solange. Let me see what she's doing in her office.

"What's up, Solange? No patients this morning?"

"Not even. I got a two o'clock. What's up with you?"

"I just had my first appointment. I got another one at 2:30. Next week, they got me working in the emergency room."

"You too? That's cool. I guess we'll be there together. What did you do last night, Anessa?"

"I went out with Alex. We went to a sex-toy party at the The HighBar."

"Did you come up on any new gadgets?"

"Of course I did. I got this ten-inch thing that sticks to the wall."

"Hold on, girl. You mean to tell me that they have a toy that sticks to the wall and I could just bend down like I'm taking it from behind?"

"I said the same thing when I laid eyes on it. I told Alex that I need that!"

"What else did you get?"

"I got a couple of flicks to watch and some ben-wa balls."

"Ben-wa balls, what the hell are those?"

"You know, the big balls with the string running through them."

"Anessa, you are a genuine freak. Is that the Asian side of you or the Dominican side of you?"

"I believe it's both sides. Every female has some freak in them. You don't deal with toys?"

"Nah, I haven't. I pleasure with myself in the shower a few times a week. Next time there's a party like that, you gotta let me know. I could use the wall toy. What are you doing for lunch?"

"I don't have no plans. Why, what's up?"

"I got my sugar daddy bringing me some food from Coast Café in Cambridge. He's supposed to bring me a plate and smoke me up during the break. I'll tell him to bring you a plate, and I'll let him know that you are gonna blow with us too."

"Are you sure he would be cool wit that, Solange?"

"Anessa, you already know, a goon will do anything for some good pussy. I haven't given him any yet either. I'm not gonna lie; I gave him head for no more than five minutes the other day. That was just a tease. I didn't let him cum or nothing like that. After I noticed that he was getting into it, trying to grab the back of my head and control me, I stopped. He's been spending money on me for about two months now. I told myself when he hits the $10,000 mark that I would give him a taste of oral pleasure. He has been satisfying me orally for a while now."

"Do you plan on letting him penetrate you?"

"Yeah, as soon as he gets to the $20,000 mark. I got a man at home that be hitting my walls the right way. I don't give up my goods to no other man unless he's spending gwop on my ass."

"I can dig that."

109

Finally, it was lunchtime. Solange and I headed out the hospital to meet her sugar daddy on Mass Avenue. When we got to Mass Avenue, she spotted the vehicle. He was behind the wheel of a candy-apple-red

S-550. This car was sweet. It made me think about trading my Beamer for one of those. Solange opened her door and introduced us to each other. Then I opened the back door and climbed in to make myself comfortable. His name was Ray Ray. He wasn't cute at all. He definitely looked like he had a quarter of a million dollars of diamonds on every part of his body. Solange got a fly-ass man at home that would do anything for her. Some women are just like guys. Actually, over the years I have realized that *"I love you"* doesn't mean shit. Coming from a woman's perspective,

I've seen it. Plus, I got a few dudes I used to be good friends with who used to tell me everything.

I kick it with a few dudes. I guess I'm not looking for Mr. Right, but at the same time, I'm a bachelorette, I'm not ready to be locked down. I love having intercourse, but I'm not gonna just go around riding everybody.

Especially with all these sexually transmitted diseases floating around. These condoms aren't 100 percent safe, and I'm definitely straight with wearing a female condom. I tried one of those with one of my partners in college. That was the worst ever. It was so uncomfortable sticking that inside me. The sensation of having unprotected sex is phenomenal. For me to do that with a man, I have to be in a relationship with him, and we both have to get tested for everything twice. If one of these dudes were to give me something that hurts when I go to the bathroom, I will make sure I cut them.

"You guys' food is in the brown paper bag behind my seat. What's your nationality, Anessa?" Ray Ray asked.

"Vietnamese and Dominican," I replied.

"I never heard of the two mixed together. Solange, here; light this blunt."

"What type of smoke is it?" Solange asked.

"Platinum Kush," Ray Ray replied.

Solange lit the cigar. I have never smoked out of a cigar. I'm so used to smoking out of my bong or my bowl. The aroma from the cigar smelled so good. After Solange took a few pulls, she handed it to me. I placed my lips on the cigar and took a deep pull. Before I exhaled, I took another pull. I let the smoke hit my lungs and then blew out the remainder of it. I continued to take a couple of drags. I would have never thought that smoking a blunt would taste this good. I handed the blunt to Ray Ray, and he told me he was good. I ended up passing it back to Solange. We continued to pass the cigar back and forth until it was done. I realized that we were sitting in front of Boston City Hospital. I grabbed the bag of food as I thanked Ray Ray for the food and smoke.

"Nice meeting you, Ray Ray. I'll see you upstairs, Solange."

CHAPTER 4

(SEAN SPEAKS)

I just finished doubling my verse in the booth. I came to the studio to lay down a chorus for my man Flash from N.B.S. He wanted me to hop on the remix to his new single. Besides that, I was making a show CD for my upcoming show at the Middle East in Cambridge. I went to the studio that I've been messing with for years on Newbury Street called Cyber Sounds. I came through with two people. My man Lil' Haiti gave me a ride with my home girl Kareema. Lil' Haiti was a cool-ass Haitian cat I spent a lot of time with in the past, rolling dice with head to head. We would usually play craps. He's married with a kid. He's actually one of the dudes I know who is actually faithful to his woman, supposedly. He's a working man. He works overnight as a supervisor at UPS.

Kareema, she's one of my homies. She goes to Fisher College also. She be throwing girls at me all day who go to her school. After I got the show CD and the song that I just recorded done, I paid for my studio time then exited the building.

"Eh yo, Sean. This show better be crazy like the one you had in Miami," Lil' Haiti said.

"You already know I'm gonna get it poppin'," I replied.

"You know I got a bunch of promiscuous women coming to see you perform, Sean," Kareema commented.

"We'll see."

"I know that your skinny ass isn't doubting a chick."

"It's too late at night to be trying to clown me, you Saudi Arabian gummy bear."

"Whatever, Sean. You look like you've been messing with dawg food!"

Lil' Haiti started to laugh uncontrollably at the mention of heroin.

"Very amusing, huh? You got the nerve to be laughing at Kareema's corny-ass jokes, you purple bastard. You look like an oil spill with teeth."

"C'mon, Sean. You are messing up my high. You are just as dark as me," Lil' Haiti said.

"Yeah, sure. Buddy."

"Where do you want me to drop you?"

"At my spot. I hope you didn't get offended by the jokes."

"You play too much, man. It's all good."

"Lil' Haiti, stop acting like a female and suck it up. You are a dark dude. So what you look like Grace Jones with cornrows? You got a wife and a kid. You got your shit together. Relax, brother," Kareema said.

"Both of y'all can rot in hell. Get out, Sean. I believe we are at your destination."

"Good looking out. I'll holla at y'all tomorrow."

I slid out of Lil' Haiti's Ford Contour. As I headed toward my building, my cell phone started to ring. "Hello?" I said. "What's up, Sean?" Jazelle asked. "He just went to work. Are you gonna come over here and let me pop you off?" "Only if you put my balls and my joint in your warm mouth at the same time."

"Without a doubt. I want you to bust on my face."

"Say no more. I'm hopping in a cab now." I got off the phone then waved the first cab that I saw. The cab pulled over instantly. "Where are you heading?" the cab driver asked. "To Esmond Street in Dorchester."

"That will be $20.00 up front."

I reached in my pocket and gave him $30.00. I'm tired of this racist shit. These cab drivers out here in Boston always think that we are gonna hop the cab. It's all good. I don't even know why I'm thinking about this dumb shit for. I got this cute chubby Puerto Rican who can suck a baseball through a straw from McDonald's. She had some fly little feet and nice toes. She was extremely thick with a fat ass. I never cracked it yet. This may sound a little messed up, but I would feel a little too funny.

Jazelle is Lil' Haiti's wife. Last week was the first time that she served my sacks. She called me out of the blue and told me that she got my number out of Lil' Haiti's phone. She caught me on one of those horny drunk nights after the club. I wanted to crash it bad, but I didn't want to do that to my man. Getting neck from her was bad enough.

The cab driver took a left turn on Esmond Street from Blue Hill Avenue.

"You can let me out here." I climbed out of the cab and closed the door. I reached for my cell phone to call her, but I already peeped her at the front door. I walked up the steps as she let me into my man's crib. I closed the door and locked it behind me. I followed her up the stairs to my man's bedroom. She had four gigantic scented candles that smelled fruity as hell. She was playing music from Spotify.

"Take off your sneakers, baby. Are those sneakers or shoes?" Jazelle asked.

"Whatever you want them to be."

"They look expensive. Is that material crocodile or alligator?"

"It's alligator."

"What are those called? You look like you paid almost $800 for them."

"Nah, I paid a little less. They're Jimmy Choo's."

"That's cool. Always looking fly. Take off your $500 jeans so I can fold them up, papi. I know you don't want them to get wrinkled."

You know I wasn't trying to let those get wrinkled. After I took the jeans off of my ass, she ripped my boxers off. She wasted no time throwing all of me into her mouth. Immediately she did exactly what I asked her to do. She lurped my ball bag and my joint into her mouth at the same time repeatedly.

"Damn, Jazelle. Why did you do it to me like I asked?"

"Because I love your shit, papi." She continued to go crazy on me. I have never seen a female so into serving a brother's sacks. It took me five minutes to squeeze off a lemon. She continued to top me off even after I busted. I guess she took my seeds down her throat like a champ.

"When I make you bust again, I want it all over my face." She continued to blow me. I had no problem gushing all over her grill.

Goddamn, two minutes later, my left knee started to buckle. Then my entire body became weak.

"Jazelle, I'm about to bust." She started licking the tip of my head and hitting her wet tongue rapidly as she stroked my manhood. I let my load go all over her lips, inside her nose, and all over her eyelids and her hair.

CHAPTER 5

(ANESSA-WOO SPEAKS)

I looked into the mirror one more good time to make sure that every bit of me was on point. I had my navy-blue jeans on with a hot pair of navy-blue Gucci stilettos I just got from Neiman's yesterday. For a top, I had a white button-up that displayed a lot of cleavage. I threw on my white rabbit fur and exited my house after putting on my lip gloss. It was a sunny afternoon, so I put my Versace Aviators on my face.

I decided to walk to the restaurant where I was meeting my date. I knew that there wouldn't be any parking available, and besides, it was literally three blocks away from my house. I was meeting this handsome black man named Sincere. I promised him that I would let him take me out this week. I told him that I had a man when I met him. I do that from time to time when I meet a man in the club. It's easier for them to understand that no means no when you say you got a man. He told me that he had a table reserved on Newbury Street at the Giorgio Armani restaurant. I have always walked past there. I just never made it inside before. I'm definitely feeling a little bit hungry.

I wonder what's on the menu, I thought.

When I got in front of the restaurant, a bright red Ferrari pulled alongside the restaurant. A tall brown-skinned man gave some money to the valet. This man was looking sharp. He had on an all-white suit with a pair of pony-fur boots. I wasn't sure what brand the shoes or the suit were, but it definitely looked hella expensive to me. His stunna shades were definitely hot. Off the back, I could tell that they were designer. His waves were spinning all the 90 way around his head so neatly. He caught eye contact with me just as he was about to walk into the restaurant.

"Good evening, sweetie. Damn! You look so edible right now," Sincere said.

"Oh, stop it. You don't mean that."

We gave each other a hug and then walked into the restaurant together. This place looked really jazzy and bougie. Sincere told the hostess his name for our reservation. Two seconds later, she walked us over to our table. The tablecloths were made out of red velvet. This place was definitely cozy and romantic.

"Have you been here before, Anessa?" Sincere asked me.

"No, I haven't. I'm really digging the ambiance in here."

"Yeah, I figured this spot might be something that you might be feeling. Wait till you try the food."

I started to look at the menu. I couldn't believe how expensive the drinks were. It cost $125 for a shot of Louis the 13th and almost $2,000 for the damn bottle. That's really inhumane.

"What would you like to drink?" Sincere asked.

"I'll take a double shot of Louis the 13th. What would you like to order?"

"A glass of Muscato and a double shot of Remy. Do you know what you want to eat?"

"Yes, I like the sound of the calamari plate with the Kobe steak."

"I was feeling the same way, to tell you the truth."

The waitress came to the table, allowing us to place our order.

"So Anessa, can I ask you a question, sweetie?"

"Of course, you can ask me anything you want."

"When are you gonna sit on my face?"

I couldn't believe Sincere asked me a bold question like that. I almost spit out my water onto the table.

"Sit on my face! What do you mean by that, Sincere?"

"Anessa, how much bolder do you want me to get? I want your swanson in my face."

"My swanson ..." I chuckled. *Swanson? What in the hell?* All I can do is laugh at that word. I got to use that word in a sentence once a day.

The waitress came to the table with our drinks just in time. I really didn't wanna answer that question. There was nothing wrong with Sincere. I just knew that if I let him taste my goods, he wouldn't stop until I gave him the business. I knew that I didn't want to have intercourse with him. Would I let him eat me out? Nah, I think that I would just continue to go on dates with him and let him spend bread on me. Twenty minutes later, our food was steamy hot in front of our faces.

"Do you want another double shot?" Sincere asked me.

"Yes, please."

"Can we please get two more shots of Louis?" Sincere asked the waitress.

"No problem," the waitress replied.

I blew on my mashed potatoes and then decided to take a taste with my fork. "Not bad."

"So what's up? You still never answered my question that I asked you over twenty minutes ago."

"And what was that question again, I'm sorry?"

"When are you gonna ride my face?"

"Oh, that question. C'mon, Sincere. I told you my situation. You know that I live with my man."

"I hear you, but I don't see a boulder drippin' from your finger."

"What do you mean by that?"

"I don't see no ice or nothing symbolizing your marriage."

"Because I'm not married yet."

"So you couldn't picture my face six inches below your pelvis?"

"Why are you talking to me like that while I'm eating?"

"I'm sorry, Anessa. You're right." Wow, I couldn't believe how bold and nasty this pervert was. I don't care how much money he threw my way. I would never let him smell my juices. The waitress placed the check book down on the table with Sincere's credit card. I tried to add up the bill in my head without looking at it. The bill was a couple of dollars shy from $1,000. We finished drinks and exited the restaurant.

"So what's up, Anessa? What are you about to get into?"

"I'm about to go to my girlfriend's house around the corner to handle a few things. Thanks a lot for the dinner and the drinks. I really enjoyed it."

"Do you need a ride?"

"No, that's okay. I'll be fine, thanks."

"Well, when will I be able to see you again?"

"You got my number. I always answer your phone calls."

"True. Come here." I walked toward him as he pulled me close to his body to embrace me. As he hugged me, he tried to be smooth and kiss me on my lips. He was too slow making the move. I observed his whole game from the moment he pulled me toward him. I could tell that he was upset that I didn't give him any tongue by the way he walked to the valet.

CHAPTER 6

(SEAN SPEAKS)

"I can't believe that y'all got me smoking out of a bong every day," I commented. "That's crazy."

"Why's that crazy, Sean? It's much more natural and better for you than that Philly blunt stuff that you brothers choose to smoke,"

Zachery replied.

"Phillies! Who the hell smokes Phillies? I haven't smoked a Philly since high school. None of my people smoke Phillies."

"What do you brothers smoke?" Cornelius asked.

"Vanilla Dutch Masters or the grape dutches. Most of the women in Boston like to smoke backwoods."

"I just think that there is way too much paper on a cigar. I used to smoke joint papers with my father. I got him smoking out of a bowl now. I can't tolerate papers," Zachery said.

"Zachery, did you tell Sean about the kegger?" Cornelius asked.

"The kegger?" I said.

"Oh yeah, the kegger. I didn't get a chance to tell him yet," Zachery said.

"What's the kegger, Cornelius?" I asked.

"When the weather got a little nicer, we was planning on throwing a keg party on the balcony."

"Have you guys thrown one before?"

"Ha ha, no. We've participated in a bunch of them before," Cornelius replied.

"How would you promote it?"

"I guess on Social Media."

"Oh, you got a Instagram page?"

"Ah , ha ha, yeah! Doesn't everybody got a Instagram page?"

"Actually, I don't have one."

"Are you serious, brother?" Zachery asked.

"You gotta be kidding me, Sean. Aren't you an artist? Every artist has a Instagram page," Cornelius said.

"I never really messed with the Internet like that. Plus, I never had anyone that would build me a Instagram page."

"Well, today is your lucky day. We are gonna build you a page right now. Do you have any pictures of you downloaded on your phone?"

"As a matter of fact, I just did a photo shoot the other day."

"Do you have that file with you now?"

"Yeah, it's in my room. Let me grab it right quick." As I walked into my bedroom, I heard the doorbell ring. I was hoping that one of these geeks had some pork coming through. I was starting to wonder if the two of them were getting any poon action. Three minutes later, I came back in the living room and seen that

Big was lounging on the couch. He had a gallon of Hennessey. He had the big joint with the handle. Plus, he was breaking up some bud.

Zachery was coming back in the room with four glasses.

"What's up, Big? What's poppin' with you?" I asked.

"Ain't nothing, man. Came to check y'all for a little bit. I just grabbed some Barney from them N.B.S. cats in the bridge."

"Ha ha, Barney! What's Barney?" Cornelius asked.

"Purple Haze. I call it Barney."

"Out of all the names out there, why would you choose a name like Barney?"

"Ah, ha ha, yea."

"Well, what color is he?"

"I don't know. He always has his costume on. Why, is he black?"

"Cornelius, what are you, mild? The man is purple. The marijuana is called Purple Haze. Therefore, in street code, to disguise the controlled substance on the phone or in code, he's using the word *Barney*," Zachery said.

"Oh, okay. Ha ha, I get it now. What's that you're spinning, a Philly? Oh, I forgot that brothers don't smoke Phillies in the ghetto no more. Is that a Dutch?"

"Yeah. What are you doing? Playing with the gram?" Big asked.

"Yeah, I'm creating Sean a page."

"It's about time, Henny. You should've been had a page. That's a good idea."

"I know. I just never had no one to build it for me."

"So, do you want to use the name Sean Winston?" Cornelius asked while he took a sip of the cognac that Big poured him.

"You already know."

"So where are you from?"

"Put Boston."

"Let me see that file with your pictures."

"It's right there next to the keyboard."

"Oh, all right. I see it." Cornelius put the usb drive in the laptop. I was kind of amped up that I was about to have a Instagram page.

"You gotta be kidding me, Sean," Big stated.

"What?"

"You are taking this tight look way too far in these pictures. I don't care if those cost $400 or not. How do girls be throwing swanson atchu wearing them snug-as-denim spandex? You can't even put your hand in your back pocket to reach for a wallet. You can't even take a seat and relax comfortably without your sacks murdering you."

"You think these chicks would rather holla at a dude that got his pants saggin' to his ankles? We are grown men now. It's time to get your grown man on."

"Whatever! Grown man? Shitttt! With them tight-ass jeans, I would have thought that you was having an identity crisis. I was thinking that you thought you was a promiscuous female in high school trying to impress the basketball players in the hallway." Everybody started to laugh at Big's jokes. I was ready to cut his fat ass up.

"Big, you must be heated that you couldn't put one of your four legs in the biggest pair of Gucci jeans, you four-legged mammal, you short-armed bag of plantains. How the hell do you wipe your ass and your box. Your balloon knot must smell like dumpster juice and catfish, you stuffed salamander."

"Whatever! Let's get back to these pictures and your snug swagger. In that picture, all the way to the left, tell me what the hell were you doing with them tight-ass jeans with that chain on your belt? How long did it take you to put on your niece's hoodie with all that glitter and cubic zirconia? You look like Ronnie from Bell Biv Devoe in '88. You also look like you belong in one of these rock groups, and you definitely got some fructose in your tank." I knew that I had to end it. Big was never gonna stop.

"All right, Big, you got me."

"Brother, I don't got you. You got you looking like a feminine rock star from Pakistan. All right, I'll let you live."

Everyone continued to laugh and drink as Cornelius finished up my page. I gave him my CD and chose five of my hottest songs to put on. "Eh yo, Sean. I almost forgot I got something for you," Big said.

"What now?"

"Damn, family. Why it gotta be like that? I'm trying to enhance your pipe game."

"By doing what, Big?"

"By hitting you with a Viagra. I snatched a couple of them from this bodega in Codman Square for $20 a pop."

"What's that supposed to do for me?"

"Keep your shit rock hard all night. Your partner will go crazy if you take a half a pill twenty minutes before you crash it."

"Just a half, you don't need a whole?"

"No, trust me, you don't."

"How much I gotta give you for this?"

"Nuttin', you're good. This one is on the house, here."

"I LOVE YOU DOESN'T MEAN SHIT"

Written by
Surpaul Cottrell

AVAILABLE NOW

"LESSONS"

THE TOOLS TO A HEALTHIER LIFE, BUSINESS, AND FUTURE

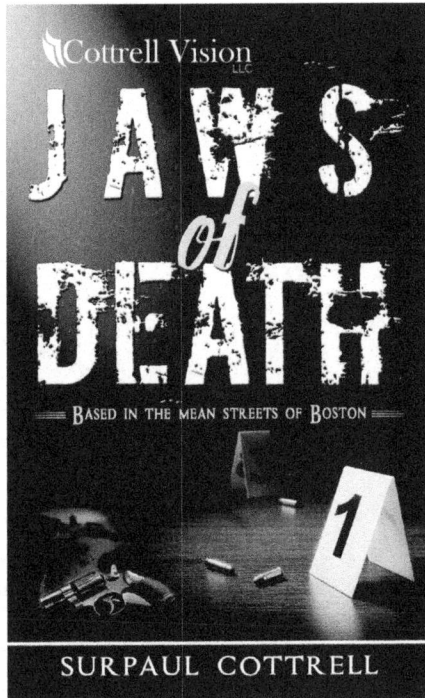

Made in United States
North Haven, CT
01 March 2022